# YOU'RE
# DOING IT
# WRONG!

# YOU'RE DOING IT WRONG!

## How to Improve Your Life by

FIXING EVERYDAY TASKS

You *(and Everyone Else)* Are Totally Screwing Up

Lee Thornton

Avon, Massachusetts

Published by
Adams Media, a division of F+W Media, Inc.
57 Littlefield Street, Avon, MA 02322. U.S.A.
*www.adamsmedia.com*

ISBN 10: 1-4405-4416-6
ISBN 13: 978-1-4405-4416-3
eISBN 10: 1-4405-4524-3
eISBN 13: 978-1-4405-4524-5

Printed in the United States of America.

10   9   8   7   6   5   4   3   2   1

This publication is designed to provide accurate and authoritative information with regard to the subject matter covered. It is sold with the understanding that the publisher is not engaged in rendering legal, accounting, or other professional advice. If legal advice or other expert assistance is required, the services of a competent professional person should be sought.
—From a *Declaration of Principles* jointly adopted by a Committee of the American Bar Association and a Committee of Publishers and Associations

Many of the designations used by manufacturers and sellers to distinguish their product are claimed as trademarks. Where those designations appear in this book and Adams Media was aware of a trademark claim, the designations have been printed with initial capital letters.

*This book is available at quantity discounts for bulk purchases.*
*For information, please call 1-800-289-0963.*

# Contents

## HEALTH AND FITNESS

Avoiding Germs on an Airplane ............................ 13

Drinking Coffee ....................................................... 16

Spot Training............................................................ 18

Tanning...................................................................... 20

Offsetting Time Spent Sitting ............................... 23

Wearing Headphones............................................... 26

Cutting Sugar ........................................................... 29

Riding Your Bike ..................................................... 32

Flattening Your Abs ................................................ 35

Timing Your Sleep ................................................... 37

Restricting Calories.................................................. 40

Staying Warm ........................................................... 42

Pooping...................................................................... 44

Brushing Your Teeth ............................................... 47

Sitting ........................................................................ 49

## SOCIAL AND FUN

Tweeting and Facebook Updating ........................... 53

Having Difficult Conversations............................... 57

Watching 3D Movies................................................. 60

Getting Revenge ....................................................... 63

Winning..................................................... 67

Sharing Your Goals ................................. 71

Giving and Receiving Compliments....................... 74

Speaking................................................ 77

Taking Pictures ....................................... 80

Talking on Your Cell Phone ....................... 83

Traveling Internationally........................... 86

## FOOD AND BEVERAGE

Measuring Flour ..................................... 93

Choosing Produce ................................... 95

Homebrewing Beer................................. 98

Choosing and Using Knives ..................... 101

Roasting Vegetables................................ 104

Eating Sushi .......................................... 107

Serving Wine......................................... 110

Tapping a Keg ........................................ 113

Tipping at Restaurants.............................. 116

Using Utensils ....................................... 120

## WORK AND FINANCE

Wearing Business Casual........................... 125

Hiring People ........................................ 128

Facing Deadlines..................................... 131

Increasing Productivity ............................ 134

Putting in Longer Hours........................... 137

Saving Money ........................................................ 140

Paying Off Your Credit Cards ............................... 143

Multitasking ......................................................... 146

Buying Happiness ................................................. 149

Negotiating .......................................................... 153

Visualizing Positively ........................................... 156

## RELATIONSHIPS AND SEX

Kissing ................................................................. 161

Dealing with a Breakup ........................................ 164

Handling Romantic Jealousy ................................. 167

"Working On" Your Relationship .......................... 170

Texting Your Partner ............................................ 173

Protecting Yourself Against STDs ......................... 176

Online Dating ...................................................... 179

Speed Dating ........................................................ 182

## HOME AND AUTO

Removing Stains from Clothing ............................. 187

Using WD-40 ....................................................... 190

Training Your Dog ................................................ 192

Feeding Your Cat .................................................. 195

Taking Care of Your Lawn .................................... 198

## RESOURCES

RESOURCES .......................................................... 201

# Introduction

We do things wrong all the time, of which we are well aware. We take shortcuts and risks, but they are often calculated, even subconsciously, as we weigh "good" and "bad" choices, and sometimes choose "bad" for time management, affordability, or even just for fun. The trouble comes in when we accidentally tip the scales, making "bad" choices we *think are good!* Not because we're stupid, but because logic, experts, and beloved family members told us so. (Okay, for some people, it's because they're stupid.) Now you have this handy guide to help you out with those sticky issues. From airplanes and abs to watching 3D and winning, get ready to do it right!

# HEALTH
# AND
# FITNESS

# Avoiding Germs on an Airplane

## The air is just fine. Your tray table and aisle seat, on the other hand . . .

You're nestled upon your airplane pillow, in your aisle seat for easy access to the bathroom so you can wash your hands frequently to keep all those airplane germs at bay. This may shock you, Dr. Pasteur, but you're doing it wrong. In fact, you're probably exposing yourself to more germs than when using a sunbaked Porta-Potty at a summer music festival*. (*data pending)

How about if you're really hard-core about germs, and you brought a little mask to breathe through? If you've ever worn one for more than five minutes, you know how uncomfortable they get. But it's worth it not to get sick, right? All the recirculated air is full of germs, right? You've worked in an office, and you lived in a huge dorm. You know about these things. So you decide to go wash your hands and have a little snack on your tray table. The problem is, you're disgusting.

**HOW TO DO IT RIGHT**

## Touch as little as possible, and move to the window seat

First of all, don't worry about the air; it's the least of your problems (especially if you're actually wearing the surgeon's mask). Airplane air is only partially recirculated. Boeing's website states, of its commercial planes: "Air circulation is continuous. Air is always flowing into and out of the cabin." That means most commercial buildings on the ground have dirtier air than your airplane's cabin.

Pillows and blankets are often recycled, so be sure to avoid those. A highly germ-laden surface is your seatback tray table. In a 2007 study, Jonathan Sexton found 60 percent of airplane tray tables were positive for Methicillin-resistant Staphylococcus Aureus (MRSA). Sexton recommends using antibacterial wipes on the tray before you even think about eating off it.

As for the hand washing, airplane bathrooms are crammed with contaminants—some studies found that even the running *sink water* itself occasionally contained fecal bacteria. The bathroom sinks are also loaded with bacteria—their small size forces many people to touch the rims of the sinks with their dirty hands. If you have a short flight, use the restroom before you board and avoid the airplane bathroom entirely. If that's not reasonable, be sure to carry hand sanitizer with you, so you can sanitize even after you wash your hands.

Now on to that convenient aisle seat—it's the most dangerous choice when it comes to airplane germs, as it is touched the most and, therefore, is the most likely to have been contaminated. Studies by the Centers for Disease Control have found that in a plane in which some passengers are ill, the people sitting in the aisle seats were most likely to contract the same illness. Luckily, there are several ways to get yourself a window seat: book early, and confirm your seat when booking, and again when you check in. Join a frequent flier program, as seat selection is often part of the program's rewards. In some cases, you can upgrade your seat for a fee (Continental, JetBlue, and Virgin America all offer fee-based seat upgrades per flight, and United offers an annual fee option.) Get to the airport early to ensure you don't lose your spot, and if all else fails—ask. Remember to be nice to the often-maligned staff, and at the last minute, they may be able to move you into the seat of a no-show. If you're rude or demanding, there's very little chance they will go out of their way to help you.

Don't be shy about taking out the Handi Wipes and wiping down your surfaces, and using hand sanitizer, even if it makes you look a little neurotic. If you're concerned about the chemicals, tea tree or neem oil wipes from your local health food store are helpful. Don't forget the 3.4-ounce rule on liquids, so don't bring your jug of sanitizer from the BigLots store. You really don't need more than 3 ounces. If you do—you're doing it wrong. And hey, at least you're not wearing a mask!

# Drinking Coffee

## Too much, too fast, too often

Mornings come easy to some people, but the rest of us drag out of bed and immediately look forward to a large coffee, and we keep chugging away throughout the day. Perhaps you prefer soda or iced tea, but every time you start to feel sluggish, it's time for another hit of caffeine! But be warned: That delicious comfort drink of the ages is actually making you more tired.

## Slow and steady wins the race

Some doctors would say to cut caffeine out entirely, but let's be realistic here and listen to some professionals who advise how to do caffeine right: The secret is small amounts throughout the day.

The reason that first morning coffee feels *so good* is because you're actually avoiding caffeine withdrawal with each sip. A 2004 study at Johns Hopkins analyzed 170 years (seriously, that goes back to before the Civil War) of caffeine withdrawal information to discover caffeine withdrawal is an actual, medical *thing*. The delight a substantial caffeine user gets from that morning coffee is actually just a cessation of withdrawal symptoms.

As you go about your day, your body keeps building its store of adenosine, a nifty little enzyme that makes your body sleepy. Caffeine blocks this process. Sounds like you can fool your body ad infinitum and keep blocking those receptors and never sleep, right? Well, the problem with that is you're producing *more* sleepiness receptors if you drink caffeine on a regular basis. So you're stuck with more receptors that result in you waking up in the morning with your body complaining to you rather loudly that you really should sleep, not work.

Also, as you pump in more and more caffeine, it tells the nerve receptors to speed up. So although it's great you got so much work done in the last hour, it's a finite thing—too much and you've crossed the fine line of neuron-firing. Your brain gets a signal that something is wrong, and now your pupils are dilated, your heart races, your airways open, and blood diverts to your muscles to aid you in your choice of fight or flight. And after that mess, you're going to be tired, in what is often called a "caffeine crash."

Other studies have found the delicate balance between using caffeine and being used by caffeine.

A 2004 study by James K. Wyatt in the journal *SLEEP* found using small amounts of caffeine throughout the day to be the most effective for alertness, far more effective than ingesting a full cup in the morning and another shortly after, and another . . . you get the idea. The recommendation that came out of this research: You should drink caffeine slowly.

Dr. Emily Senay, a medical correspondent for CBS's *The Early Show*, reiterated that a big coffee in the morning is a poor choice. "As the day goes on," Senay said, "we get drowsier and drowsier. When we really need the caffeine, it's not in our system, which is later in the day."

Slow and steady might win the race after all. And if you've been guzzling, slowly lowering your amount of caffeine consumed will spare you the withdrawal side effects.

# Spot Training

## Trying to lose fat in a specific area with spot training on machines

You head into the gym. You decide to work trouble areas such as your abs and build up your arms on the shiny machines with weight stacks that focus on a specific area. You adjust the weights to your number, pushing a little more each time. You're not getting your ideal definition, but it takes a while, right? Wipe down the sweat you didn't break and leave that machine for the next person—that's right; you're spot training wrong.

## Turn it up a notch

Work harder and engage your core is the more straightforward answer to the spot training problem. For advice on spot training, who better to ask than J. T. Netterville, the State Director for the National Strength and Conditioning Association of Hawaii? That's right, Hawaii, the state where bikini bods are on display year-round.

"The trouble with spot training is simple. It doesn't work," Netterville puts it bluntly. "Spot training," as we know it in the United States, is what people think of as "strength training," and people associate the words with arm curls, triceps extensions, and crunches, and mistake it for being actual *resistance* training.

Netterville describes those one-part-at-a-time fitness machines as "selectorized machines," and says they "were originally invented to make the activity of lifting weights easier." Seems counterproductive, doesn't it?

So what makes a great workout? Consider the overload principle. When the body is given more physical stress than it's accustomed to, it will attempt to accomplish the task better the next time around and generate more strength and endurance. Selectorized machines are screwing up challenging your body with those padded seats, which are actually encouraging tons of muscles to relax. Consider the chest press as an example. Netterville points out that when using a chest press, you're not forced to activiate your core muscles, your abs, or your legs. Netterville suggsts trying those same moves done with a pair of cables, and you'll feel all those sleepy muscles activate. The abs contract, the legs fight for balance and stability, and your core is engaged to maintain your posture. As you work harder, more energy burns, and as that happens, strength builds and yet more fat is burned.

Instead of targeting small muscle areas with little movements like those done on machines or even arm curls and tricep extensions with free weights, go for bigger movements that require more of your body's energy. Pull-ups, squats, pushups, lunges, and kettlebell workouts require more of your body's effort. More muscles used means more built, used, and requiring more energy, so your metabolism increases.

Selectorized machines are the result of the increased popularity of professional bodybuilding, in which an individual muscle must be worked, to be later judged for points. If that's your goal, keep working those machines. If your goal is to lose weight and/or improve your overall fitness level, however, the verdict is that one-at-a-time muscle training isn't going to help you.

# Tanning

## Going to a tanning salon . . . or not tanning at all

Thanks to the popularity of *Jersey Shore*, tanning is back, after a lengthy time as a pariah, lurking on the fringes of culture. And even though most people would never admit to wanting the "Jersey Shore Look," tans have been fashionable since Coco Chanel's accidental sunburn in the 1920s turned out to be a huge hit. *I know better*, you think to yourself. *Tans cause cancer, and the vampire look is in*. Okay, so those last two are true, but it's also true that no sun exposure is a bad choice if you are still a mortal.

## HOW TO DO IT RIGHT

## A little bit goes a long way

The worst of the worst here? Tanning beds. Unrelentingly, they're bad news in study after study, no matter how the boutiques try to spin it. The research varies, from dire death warnings to "you might need a mole cut out later," but the majority of medical professionals agrees that tanning beds are bad for your health.

As for why self-proclaimed *tanorexics* keep going back to tanning beds, a few tanning studies have produced evidence that tanning is actually addictive. In one study, frequent tanners experienced activity in their brains when exposed to UV light. When, unknown to them, the UV light was filtered out, the brains weren't fooled and no areas lit up. Those sections of the brain are the same ones associated with addiction.

Now here's where things get tricky: The American Academy of Dermatology is standing by the idea that all ultraviolet A and B rays are to be avoided, whether they come from sunlight or tanning beds. This is where the medical community gets contentious. It's hard to find actual, reputable medical professionals advocating tanning beds, but there's a whole medical community of people ready to fling their arms open and sing a refrain of "Let the Sun Shine In."

In the foreword of the book *The Vitamin D Solution* by Dr. Michael F. Holick, Dr. Andrew Weil writes, "just as we require a little fat and salt for survival, we need the sun in moderation too—for sun exposure is our best source of vitamin D." According to Dr. Holick's research, in the past decade, the American population has suffered a 22 percent loss in vitamin D, a crucial hormone for health.

Dr. Frank Lipman recommends fifteen to thirty minutes in the sun, without sunblock, two to four times per week. To protect yourself against sun damage, he suggests you build up your "internal sunblock" with food-based antioxidants and healthy fats, such as those found in blueberries, raspberries, pomegranates, and also fish oil and powdered greens supplements.

Vitamin D's importance has become a recent hot topic in health, as studies continue to find more disease associated with deficiency, including bone problems, heart disease, and a variety of cancers. Although the American Academy of Dermatology is still recommending vitamin supplementation of vitamin D over moderate UV exposure, other doctors are pushing back. Dr. Holick found 87 percent of dermatologists in sunny Australia to be vitamin D deficient. He writes, "The doctrine of dermatology will take time to rewrite, but in the meantime, each one of us can establish and follow our own canon of health."

Many have pointed to history and common sense to defend sensible exposure to the sun, such as how could our caveman ancestors have survived if the sun was such a threat? "Humans evolved in sunlight," Dr. Holick explains. "Our hunter-gatherer forbearers were making thousands of units of vitamin D every day, and our body has adapted to that need." Although sun-advocating doctors do recommend vitamin D supplements, many don't feel supplementation without sunshine is sufficient.

It's an issue your general practitioner and your dermatologist might come to blows over, but if your vitamin D levels are low at your next checkup (and make sure they are checked!), look into the research to decide what's right for you. And everyone can agree: tanning beds and especially sunburns are seriously bad for your health, with many doctors ranking them as dangerous as smoking. As for the vampire look—you know those hot *True Blood* characters are technically *dead*, right?

# Offsetting Time Spent Sitting

## A certain amount of damage simply can't be offset: Constant sitting must be avoided.

You know a sedentary lifestyle isn't healthy, so before or after work, you hit the gym. You even work out more than your doctor's recommendation of twenty to thirty minutes five times a week. And on the weekends, there's Ultimate Frisbee, pickup kickball games, and long, slow walks on the beach at sunset. Did you mention the company's softball league? You're practically Jack LaLanne. Those eight hours a day in the office spent sitting on your butt are more than accounted for.

Only . . . it turns out all that sitting technically can't be "offset." The physical activity is great and does contribute immensely to your health, but sitting all day is still chipping away at your survival odds.

## Don't just sit there

Don't sit all day. Those ergonomic exercises you do once a day aren't enough, either. Talk to your boss about getting a standing desk, or be industrious like the many bloggers who documented their various offices and their desks hoisted up to standing levels by reams of paper, cement blocks, even towers of soda cans. All because the American Cancer Society conducted a fourteen-year study that found sitting time correlated with advanced mortality rates. The study found that repercussions of sitting include obesity, diabetes, cardiovascular problems, and increased cancer risk; however, the heart issues posed the greatest risk. The worst part? No amount of exercising can reverse the damage.

So all that work you've done to "offset" your sitting time gave you a whole new range of health benefits, but it wasn't able to erase the damage caused by sitting for several hours every day.

Although no one denies hitting the gym is essential to good health, the new research gives us a bit of a jaw-dropper—you're still hurting yourself with your sitting, regardless of how awesome your calf definition is right now.

The Mayo Clinic's Dr. James A. Levine is a determined soldier against sitting. His weapon of choice in this battle: a very slow-moving treadmill. Levine created a treadmill desk in 2004, and it's finally starting to catch on. Instead of sitting at a desk, the worker stands at one . . . which is mounted to a treadmill paced to a slow walk. Mutual of Omaha, Best Buy, Google, eBay, Kraft, and GlaxoSmithKline were among the many companies that purchased Levine's Walkstations for their employees. Other walk-and-work devotees have made less pretty—but far cheaper—mash-up treadmill desks, with materials such as a used treadmill, particleboard, insulation foam, and spray paint.

Even though standing without walking may burn fewer calories, it protects you from the health risks of sitting for more than four hours a day. By elevating your desk to standing height, you open the door to improved posture and increased productivity. Those who have tried it recommend investing in good running shoes and a rubber mat to stand on. Take sit-down breaks and expect about a week before it feels comfortable. The first few days can be tough, so be prepared for some breaking-in time.

Much like workouts, a standing or walking desk will leave you with a trimmer physique, but the even greater benefits are the ones you can't see. And your colleagues shouldn't be snickering at your weird standing desk when you're looking *so* much better than them.

# Wearing Headphones

## HOW YOU'RE DOING IT WRONG

Wearing them too often and in situations where you need to hear your environment. Yes, you.

You and your tunes are inseparable. Whether it's Coachella's annual lineup or Tuvan throat singers, you don't mess around when it comes to music. You don't go anywhere without your iPod and those tiny, unobtrusive earbuds with miraculous powers of volume. Or maybe you're more into old-school ear-covering headphones with outside noise cancellation technology. Either way, you're doing it wrong.

## HOW TO DO IT RIGHT

Tune in (less frequently) and turn it (way) down

First of all, stop wearing them so much. Secondly, stop wearing them while walking around places where you need to hear things like honking horns, or yes, train whistles. If that sounds obvious, it's not obvious enough because accidental deaths of pedestrians wearing earphones has tripled since 2004.

A study led by Dr. Richard Lichenstein focused on 116 cases of accidents (70 percent of which were fatal) of headphone-wearers near roads and train stations. The study found that in thirty-four of the cases honking or sirens were actually recorded before collision with the victim. More than one-third of the case studies involved people under the age of eighteen, and two-thirds were under thirty.

"Auditory cues can be more important than visual ones" in a pedestrian situation, the study stated, referring to "nonattention blindness"—a lack of awareness of one's surroundings due to diverted attention when using headphones, and increasing your chances of "missing cues" that danger is afoot.

Although you may think such mistakes are for teenagers and not you, the statistics show all earphone-wearers are at risk, no matter how wise we think we are now. Wearing headphones is a form of sensory deprivation, as it monopolizes hearing and tasks the brain's resources by piling on another insistent stimulus. By overloading your hearing, you may not be seeing as well either, via distraction.

Hearing specialist and author Dr. Guy Berard points out that in normal hearing, when you are walking down the street and hear the chirp of birds or the honk of a horn, those sounds pass through the atmosphere before reaching your tympanic drums, which receive the sound. The atmosphere acts as a buffer to the sound. When sound is placed directly in the ear canal with headphones (especially earbuds), Dr. Berard says, "You are hearing sounds coming directly from the membrane of the headphone to your tympanic membrane, through the one square centimeter of air included in your outer ear canal, the impact is practically direct, without any possibility of easing this aggression."

Aggression? Seriously? But you were just grooving on some gentle '70s ballads! Could it be Cat Stevens and Carole King are trying to kill you? Unequivocally, yes. Well, not them personally, but the nonaggression of the music doesn't lessen its likelihood of distracting you into missing lifesaving cues. And even if you're incredibly careful, headphones pose yet another risk: hearing damage.

A study from the Annals of Internal Medicine states that 20 percent of Americans have some form of hearing loss—a much higher number than ever encountered in the past, likely due to the way earbuds pump sound directly into our ears. Earphone users should experiment to find sound levels that are safe for their ear *and* allow them to hear sounds around them as well.

Earphone fans will disagree with the good doc, saying that their music blasting directly into their ears is good for the soul—and they may have a valid argument, albeit harder to prove scientifically. So we're best to take a mix of the doctors' advice: less time with 'em in, and volume control.

Besides all the danger, a 2005 study by Robert Morrison Crane at Humboldt State University found users of frequent "portable audio technology" reported greater loneliness than infrequent users. The study suggests that headphone users alienate those around them, decreasing the chance for conversations and other interaction. The study also found in the absence of humans to interact with, this same technology can be very comforting.

Sum up all findings and you get: Headphones are best used in moderation of volume and time worn, but are better avoided when there are other people around, especially people powering vehicles that could squash you.

# Cutting Sugar

## Your brain needs glucose to function

Sugar is bad. You've heard this your whole life, since your parents told you candy would rot your teeth (it will) and no, you couldn't have more, because it wasn't good for you. You heard all about the dangers of high-fructose corn syrup, and you switched to diet sodas. You might even feel a little guilty when you indulge in dessert. Though it's true that the Standard American Diet includes way too much sugar, health-and-diet newbies who militantly cut out all sugar and feel pretty smug about it are just as guilty of doing it wrong.

**HOW TO DO IT RIGHT**

## Stay away from excess

Sugar is one of those substances scientists are probably going to argue about forever—the different forms of it and their relative dangers or benefits. One thing is clear: Your brain needs glucose to function. That strange and complicated organ in your noggin is only 2 percent of your body weight, but it requires about 20 percent of your daily caloric intake, and it's a bit of a cookie monster.

Not all sugar is created equally (no pun intended to the sweetener . . . or was it?). Of the simple sugars, fructose is the sweetest form, followed by sucrose, glucose, and galactose. Fructose is known as fruit sugar because it's the kind of sugar that appears in fruits and other plants, such as corn, which produces the infamous high-fructose corn syrup—more on that later. Sucrose, known as table sugar, is also derived from plants, such as the sugar beet and sugarcane. Glucose is a byproduct of plants' photosynthesis, and is produced mostly by the liver. Galactose is close in configuration to glucose and is found in dairy products, some plants, and is also synthesized by the human body. Glucose is the one we're really talking about here: It's the top source of energy for your cells, and your brain needs a constant supply, even when you're asleep.

Most sugar is probably just as bad as the research keeps telling us it is, as well as the fact that most people are over-inundated with sugar, but it's important not to forget about glucose, which is in a league of its own as far as your need for it goes. If you're dieting or trying to eat more healthily, it's common to demonize all sugars, but some people got wise to the problems of glucose insufficiency when no-carb diets became popular.

Dr. Paul Jaminet became the enemy of no-carb eaters everywhere when he dared to make an argument that the body can't produce all of its needed glucose through gluconeogenesis. Every doctor can cite certain studies to make an argument for and against certain diets, but the reality remains that biology is a vast and still-unfolding science. Dr. Jaminet encourages people to look at the "big picture" view of evolution, history, and cultural differences when considering dietary science. *"It became clear that I was just eating too few carbohydrates,"* Dr. Jaminet says of his time on a no-carb diet. *"Mucus, tears, and saliva all need sugars . . . if you don't have enough glucose, you won't make a lot of mucus and you'll get dry eyes. That makes you vulnerable to infections."*

In 2012, when the American Medical Association was asked to support a tax on beverages that contain sugar, they declined. Even some doctors and nutritionists had negative reactions to the trend of putting sugar on the same level of danger as smoking or alcohol.

"Sugar does not cause obesity and diabetes," Dr. Keith Ayoob told *ABC News*. "Excess causes those, and it doesn't matter where the excess comes from. There is no evidence that these diseases are caused by a particular food or nutrient."

Given that glucose is needed by your brain, it shouldn't be a huge shock that glucose can influence your behavior. It may be a joke that dieters are cranky, but low blood sugar causing increased anger is real, and "hanger" for "hunger-anger" and "food swings" have even made it into *Urban Dictionary*. Low blood sugar triggers a shift in hormones and neurotransmitters that results in suppressing serotonin receptors, making your body less able to process mood and appetite. "Hanger" can take some less-than-pleasant aspects of your personality and exaggerate them. People prone to feeling frustrated with other life situations are more likely to have the same reaction to hunger.

So although it's great to cut complex carbs and sugars, don't go overboard and forget about your friend glucose. He just might be the one to keep you from freaking out and alienating your actual friends.

# Riding Your Bike

## Not wearing gloves to protect your ulnar nerve, and overextending your legs

You're not one of those crazy-finicky bike people, but you love your bike. You hop on and ride to work, basking in the glow of your freedom from petroleum dependence, and at the same time getting a good workout. Sure, your hands kinda hurt, and your legs kinda hurt, but that's all part of being a bike rider, right? You'll toughen up.

Turns out: you don't have to hurt your hands or legs, so if you are, you guessed it—you're riding your bike wrong.

## Take the Goldilocks approach and find a bike that's just right

One of the most common causes of pain from bike riding is riding a bike that isn't the right size for you. When sitting on a bike seat the right height for you, you should be able to almost (but not quite) extend your leg while the pedal is in the arch of your foot, meaning you should have an ever-so-slight bend in your knee when the pedal is at its lowest point.

Lance Armstrong's *Livestrong.com* site offers more helpful tips for matching your size to the correct bike size. It suggests people who are five feet tall to five feet eight inches tall should use sixteen-inch wheels; people who are five feet seven inches to six feet one inches tall should use eighteen-inch wheels, and anyone over six feet should use twenty- or twenty-one-inch wheels.

Author Frank Whittemore suggests you "stand over the top tube part of the bike, with your feet flat on the ground." If your feet aren't comfortably on the ground, the bike is too large for you. Adjust the seat so your legs are "slightly bent" as urban bicycle advocate Matthew Baume suggests. Your arms should flex slightly when reaching the handlebars with a comfortable lean forward. If you need to reach, or have a lot of flex in your elbows, the bike is the wrong size for you.

If you have soreness or tingling in your hands or fingers after riding, you probably have some compression on the ulnar nerve, also known as "handlebar palsy." Baume suggests wearing padded gloves to take the strain off the ulnar nerve, particularly when on a bumpy ride. They're not necessary for everyone, but an inexpensive investment if you are in fact experiencing hand pain.

Good point, unless you have a glove phobia (though most "glove phobias" are actually about latex or medical professionals, so you probably don't have this problem). And if you're riding in a city, or any place with rough paving, you may not have to bike very far or very often to have some ulnar nerve compression, even though you might have thought your hands just needed to "toughen up."

Although many bike riders are in the dark about proper bike fit and ulnar nerve pressure, they might be slightly aware they are doing other things wrong, but insist on doing them anyway. For safety's sake, Baume would like to point out a few. Even though we know you're totally already doing these:

- Brake early in the rain. Wet brake pads are less effective.
- White lights in front, red lights in back. Never reverse them, as that can make it look like your bike is traveling in the opposite direction.
- Always ride with traffic, never against.
- Always use hand signals.

Baume cedes that hand signals "will make you look like a dork," but "it is the law and it will help prevent drivers from killing you."

We know *you* haven't been endangering yourself and others just to look cool, but you know, tell a friend. And remember to patronize bike-friendly establishments to encourage more "bike parking." Wear a helmet, and of course, skip the earphones. Besides all the obvious— your muscles might be sore from the workout, but if your legs hurt from under or overextension— re-fit your bike. If your hands hurt, don't wait for them to "get tough," because what you really need is to protect your nerves, not to try to develop calluses. That would be doing it wrong. Now ride on and enjoy your green karma and freedom from oil dependence!

# Flattening Your Abs

## Crunch-centric core training doesn't tap into the optimal way your abdominals work

You do eight different variations on the traditional sit-up, and you know they're all superior. You know you have to work your obliques, and you crunch and twist away. But what you're doing wrong is working harder, not smarter . . . by not using your abdominals in line with their ideal function.

## Work your core the way your core was meant to work

To understand how to maximize abdominal results, let's turn to our old friend J. T. Netterville, Hawaii's State Director for the National Strength and Conditioning Association, and Teresa Tapp, exercise physiologist and creator of the proper-alignment-centric "T-Tapp" workout series.

Netterville explains: "The rectus abdominis (abs) weren't actually designed to sit the body up. They were made to keep you from falling backwards." Netterville says to test that, stand facing a friend. Put your hand on your stomach and have your friend push your shoulder—you'll feel the muscles working to keep you upright.

"The best way to train them to be stronger and more toned? Use them to function like they were meant to function."

Netterville recommends full-body movements, such as squats with weights, pushups, bent-over rows, and pull-ups. Teresa Tapp also emphasizes full-body movements in her exercises to tone the abdominal area. Tapp is focused on "cardio-kinetic" moves that are cardiovascular but also nonimpact.

Tapp encourages people to determine their body type to best flatten their stomachs. If you have a longer torso and shorter legs, your main problem may be in the lower stomach and/or a thicker waistline. If you have a shorter torso and longer legs, you have less room for your waist to "cinch in," and may have trouble getting a smaller waistline.

Tapp's workouts reflect her clinical background, and are based more in the world of wellness than weight loss. (In fact, Tapp advises people to "throw out their scales" and just trust how their clothes fit instead.) Her recommended exercises are those that work with the natural inclinations of the abdominals to sculpt them into a "natural girdle" that holds the "organs in place." Tapp's workouts are for men too, but the "organs in place" abdominal workout is especially popular with new moms. Detailed descriptions of her movements are free on her site, *www.t-tapp.com*.

Netterville says of skipping the crunches and targeted twists in favor of full-body movements that the strength goes not only to the abs, but the sides, "love handles," and back, creating more strength and burning more fat. "That's one of the most important parts for the beach body conscious crowd," he says of fat-burning. "That extra energy you're burning is all that fat covering those abs you're working so hard to sculpt."

# Timing Your Sleep

## Sticking to straight eight-hour increments, when sleep actually has repeated ninety-minute cycles

You got your eight hours of beauty rest. You know how important it is for virtually every aspect of your physical and emotional health. You make sure that as often as possible, you get to bed eight hours before the alarm goes off. So why do you feel so tired sometimes when the alarm goes off, and other times you feel all right? It depends on what time you fell asleep, because sleep goes in continuous ninety-minute cycles, not eight-hour cycles.

## Maximize your cycles

Try to time your sleep in multiple ninety-minute cycles from the time you fall asleep. For example, if you need to get up for work at 7:30 A.M., you want to fall asleep at 10:30 P.M., or 12:00 A.M., or even 1:30 A.M. to ensure you don't try to rouse yourself mid-cycle.

In *PsychDigest*, Dr. David S. Kantra described how each ninety-minute sleep cycle is a "V," if your sleep were to be made into a graph. It takes forty-five minutes to get to the deepest part of the "V," and forty-five minutes to get back up. The deeper into the "V" you are when you're awakened, the groggier you'll feel.

Although you have been taught to get your eight hours, the National Sleep Foundation stresses that there's no "magic number," and ideal hours of sleep vary from person to person.

According to *The Berkeley Science Review*, each ninety-minute cycle has five stages. Stage Five is where REM sleep and dreaming occur. However, this cycle shifts as you sleep, so in the first to second cycles, you don't get as much REM sleep as you get in your second to fifth cycles. Variations on the amount of REM sleep depend on the individual, if the sleep happened at night or in the daytime, and on age. Newborns spend half their sleep in REM, and teenagers require more sleep cycles in total than adults.

People who hate naps are probably especially sensitive to sleep cycles. That groggy feeling of trying to emerge from a deep part of your sleep cycle is known as sleep inertia, and can be common for people who try to schedule naps in forty-five-minute or one-hour increments. Some sleep experts now recommend a twenty-minute nap to reap the benefits of non-REM sleep, or a ninety-minute nap to get a full cycle. Amie Gordon points to other scientists who are beginning to take a cue from nap-happy cultures that don't fight the after-lunch lull that hits around 2:00 P.M. There's some evidence our circadian rhythms take a dip then, so humans may just be built for napping.

If you're glued to your smartphone, try an app like WakeMate to help wake you in tune with your cycles. WakeMate uses twenty-minutes cycles and an actigraph device, worn on the wrist, to collect your sleep data and determine your wake-up time by carefully monitoring the motion of your wrist as it correlates to your sleep cycling. A free sleep calculator is also available at *http://sleepyti.me* to advise you on your fall-asleep time based on your needed wake-up time.

# Restricting Calories

## By restricting your calories significantly, your metabolism drops and you store more fat

You cut down to a thousand calories a day. With that deficit in your caloric intake, your body is just going to have to feed off your fat stores, right? You can just *feel* the love handles being eaten away and used as energy by your body. Except maybe what you're feeling is your fat stores being *added to*, because your body thinks it's starving and is storing as much fat as possible.

## Make those calories count

One way to cut calories without dropping your metabolism is though calorie cycling. Certified behavioral analyst Leigh A. Richmond recommends "People who have five to twenty pounds to their goal weight can cycle between 1200 and 1700 calories on different days, eating foods with different nutrient densities to keep their bodies 'guessing' and working hard. It keeps their metabolism going full speed until their goal weight."

The main problem with the way doctors have been advising weight loss for years—by cutting 500 calories a day—has been debunked recently, as scientists have found the old advice doesn't account for the fall of metabolism as the body adjusts to the decrease in energy (calories) consumed. Professionals advise women should not consume fewer than 1,200 calories a day and men should not consume fewer than 1,500 unless supervised by a medical professional.

As for upping your protein with the calorie reduction, studies show there's no evidence that eating more than 12 to 15 percent of your calories in protein slowed fat gains. However, a cut to protein in your diet is likely to send your body into fat-storing mode. The happy medium is understanding the importance of protein, but not relying on it to speed your metabolism.

Dr. Carson Chow with the National Institutes of Health says their studies found the way to cut calories for slow but permanent weight loss was to cut only 150 calories a day.

Dr. Elizabeth McGraw, entomologist at the University of Queensland, has done studies on flies to examine the effects of calorie restriction. Of course, humans are very different than flies, yet the studies gave McGraw enough information to warn that "dietary restriction has complex effects on animals," and that calorie restriction "could have the unwanted side effect of reducing survival to infections."

Previous research on animals indicated that calorie restriction slowed aging, but those studies were done in pathogen-free environments. Researchers are now finding in "the real world," calorie restriction leaves calorie-dependent living beings vulnerable to pathogenic infection.

When you combine that information with how unpleasant dieting can be, it seems like a better weight loss plan to exercise more and just burn those extra calories!

# Staying Warm

## It's just myth that most of your body heat is lost through your head

Thermal cap? Check. Earmuffs? Check. Scarf wrapped around your neck and lower face? Check. Well, you might look ready to rob a convenience store, but this is one of those rare situations where Mom wasn't right—you're not losing 90 percent of your body heat through your head.

## Keep warm from the inside out

The hat isn't as important as insulating with the right materials—and your diet. "If it's cold outside, protect your body," advise the authors of the study to debunk the hat myth, Dr. Rachel C. Vreeman and Dr. Aaron E. Carroll. "Whether you want to keep your head covered or not is up to you."

The original study in the 1950s wasn't exactly incorrect that its subjects lost body heat through their heads, it's just misleading. The subjects involved were in arctic survival suits, with their heads uncovered, so the head was the only option for heat loss. Vreeman and Carroll write: "Had this experiment been performed with subjects wearing only swimsuits, they would not have lost more than 10% of their body heat through their heads."

Here's a secret to staying warm you might have missed while worrying about your hat: wool. Besides being cute and making funny sounds, those innocent-looking sheep are madly producing one of nature's most versatile and useful fibers with their coats. Wool can keep your body warm, it's fire resistant, wicks moisture away, is elastic, flexible, and durable. Whereas a cotton fiber breaks after about 3,000 bends, a wool fiber can endure about 20,000.

Another way to stay warm that is often overlooked is food. *Outdoor Life* writer Rich Johnson recommends if you're spending some outdoor-time in the cold, nourish yourself with "high-powered, high-caloric foods that include a balanced blend of protein, carbohydrates and fat." Johnson recommends food such as a breakfast of oat porridge mixed with fruit and seeds, or an omelet with eggs and bacon and cheese for protein, fats, and calories to keep you going in the cold. He recommends hot soup for lunch and carb-loaded pasta for dinner.

Looking for foods to keep you warm that are slightly less suited to a lumberjack? Vitamin B3, also called niacin, expands the capillaries and assists the circulatory system, meaning warmer extremities. Peanuts, sesame, milk, eggs, and cheese are sources of niacin. Protein warms us up by raising the pH of our blood. Meat, beans, tofu, and tempeh are excellent sources of protein. Spicy foods containing capsaicin can increase body temperature, so snack on spiced nuts to get both spice and healthy fat, or enjoy a hot and spicy soup.

# Pooping

## Your body is designed to eliminate waste by squatting, not sitting

This one is really simple, you learned it when you were a toddler. Sit on potty, poop, get potty treat. Okay, hopefully you're not still getting rewards for using the toilet. But even a child knows the right way to poop, right? Well, depends on the child, but for most Americans, the answer is no.

### HOW TO DO IT RIGHT

## Sit less, squat more

"We were not meant to sit on toilets," proctologist Michael Freilich famously told *TIME* magazine in 1978, after President Carter had hemorrhoid troubles. "We were meant to squat in the field."

Scientific studies across the globe confirm Freilich is correct. Many countries eschew the sitting position for defecation and squat, but in places in Asia, Europe, and the Middle East, one can find toilets designed for squatting, not sitting. Western toilets and their poor grasp of our poop-related anatomy probably explain why by age fifty, half of Americans will have experienced hemorrhoids, the dreaded swelling and sometimes bleeding of veins in the rectal cavity.

"Most of the world squats," Professor Alexander Kira told *TIME* in 1966. "It is more natural and easier on the body." The reason for this is a bit of biological geometry. Defecation isn't controlled by our sphincter muscles alone—there is a bend between the rectum and the anus, where feces are held by a 90-degree angle, called an anorectal angle. When one squats, this angle is released. A Japanese study by Dr. Ryuji Sakakibara and colleagues found that when sitting, the anorectal angle increases to 100 degrees, but it increases to 126 degrees in a squat. In addition, the researchers measured significantly less abdominal pressure in the squatters.

In a 2003 study with Israeli doctor Dov Sikirov, participants defecated sitting on a sixteen-inch-high toilet, a twelve-inch-high toilet, and squatting over a container. Sikirov found that participants' bowels moved in fifty-one seconds when squatting, but took 130 seconds on the high toilet. This is bad news for Americans, where the trend is for "comfort toilets" that are taller than ever. The "comfort" part is in relation to not having to put much effort into sitting and standing, not the "comfort" of straining one's bowels at an inferior angle.

What's the big deal with a little strain? Sakakibara's study found that squatters have fewer incidents of hemorrhoids, constipation, and diverticulosis. Reducing pressure on the lower abdomen reduces the likelihood of suffering from defecation syncope, deep vein thrombosis, and stroke, so the benefits go way beyond spending a little less time in the bathroom.

Besides the strain factor, a 2002 Iranian study by Dr. Saeed Rad found, when taking radiographs of both sitters and squatters during defecation, that squatting resulted in "more complete" and "efficient" bowel movements. So not only does squatting provide less pressure, it gets more fecal matter out of the colon.

Proponents of squat toilets speculate that your body's waste may be harboring toxic material that is best to get out of you as quickly as possible, but there's no science to support that yet, so it's still a theory.

At this point you may be wondering why people insist on Western toilets if scientists have been telling us to squat since the 1960s. Well, once again, there's no hard science on that but it seems to be both psychological and physical. In general, Americans tend to be overweight, and many are simply unable to squat for a bowel movement. Writer Amy Chavez took on the subject in *The Japan Times*, explaining to its Asian readership that "The Asian-style squat and flush is not our style. Americans like to take our time." Chavez also noted that "Japanese-style toilets require far too much physical prowess for the average American."

Chavez also noticed other Westerners confiding that they found the idea of squatting "barbaric." The psychological factor of having a vulnerable, private moment in a way so different from how we've done it our entire lives is extremely daunting for some people. Some naturopathic doctors have lamented they can't even get any patients to *speak* of their bowel habits— they're too shy. And besides the mental factor, there's the physical: the challenge of the squat. But for those who have tried it, most are converts. If you can get past your brain and your body, upgrading your home toilet is fairly simple. You can purchase devices online to make your regular toilet a squatter (see *http://squattypotty.com*) with a rather innocent-looking stool to place by the toilet to get your knees high enough for the best angle (check out *http://GoStool.com*).

# Brushing Your Teeth

## Food acids and sugars weaken your enamel, making your teeth vulnerable as you brush after eating

Maybe you just had dinner at home, so it's easy to pop into the bathroom and brush your teeth to get all that gross food-waste off them. It's a little harder when you're out and about, but you keep a travel brush in your bag, desk, or gym locker, to make sure to brush away the damage of the last meal. Except at that moment, your toothbrush is doing more harm than good.

## Hold your horses

Wait at least thirty minutes after eating before brushing. Dentist Phil Stemmer from the Fresh Breath Centre in London warns, "If you clean your teeth too soon, you are actually brushing away at the enamel before it hardens again."

Acids in foods weaken the enamel, and brushing while they are weak will wear down or scratch your enamel. Foods like citrus that have more acid leave your teeth especially vulnerable to brush-damage. Dentists recommend waiting an hour after eating before brushing, and brushing your teeth in the morning *before* breakfast, not after.

In the United Kingdom, it's estimated that 20 percent of adults have eroding enamel, partially due to over brushing. Dentists still advise you to brush twice a day, but be sure to wait after eating. And after brushing *don't rinse*, which washes away the protective layer provided by the toothpaste. A few other toothy myths include:

- *Chocolate ruins your teeth.* Sugar ruins your teeth, but chocolate has an antibacterial property that may protect your teeth. In order to get any benefit, you need to eat dark, bittersweet, real chocolate.
- *A hot pack for a toothache.* It may feel better than a cold pack at first, but heat will only add to the inflammation. Use a cold pack and get to a dentist ASAP.
- *Cavities always hurt.* Some dental decay is pain-free, as long as it is infection-free, so keep up with your dentist and don't rely on pain to signal a problem.
- *"It's just a baby tooth."* Kids' "baby teeth" may seem like nature's disposables, but losing them too soon due to decay can cause issues with chewing and "drifting" of the other baby teeth, interfering with the adult teeth coming in straight.
- *Bad teeth are always genetic.* Although the thickness of your enamel may have come from a parent, dental hygiene habits are taught at a young age, and poor dental hygiene is often passed on as well (but blamed on genetics alone).
- *White teeth are the healthiest.* Studies show as the blood supply to teeth decreases with age, the dentine below the enamel may appear to be more yellow, but these yellow teeth are more decay-resistant than naturally whiter teeth.

# Sitting

## You're turning your spine into an accordion by sitting upright in your office chair

A chair . . . you sit in it. Really, there's not much more basic than that—even the best way to stand and walk are more talked about than sitting and chairs. Hard as it is to believe, until the last two hundred years or so, sitting on a straight-backed chair was an activity reserved for the wealthy elite. If the masses wanted to sit, they had to pull up a stool, a stone, or whatever was most readily available. And, as it turns out in this case, *they were smarter than we are today.*

### HOW TO DO IT RIGHT

## Forget what your mom said about sitting up straight

Ever wonder why up to 80 percent of Americans suffer from some form of chronic back pain? Our bodies are simply not designed for the rigid right angle of the average chair.

When you're standing up, or even sitting on something backless, your abdominal muscles are active, helping your spine support your weight. When you're sitting on a chair, these muscles relax, and suddenly your spine alone has to take the entire weight of your upper torso, like a twig holding up a bowling ball. The extra stress puts constant pressure on your spine, giving you a heaping portion of daily pain by middle age.

The position that avoids any stress on ligaments is lying on your back with your knees slightly bent, which is just a slight knee bend away from the yoga pose *Savasana*—also known delightfully as "corpse pose." It's wonderful in a yoga practice between challenging poses, but it's definitely not conducive to getting, say, office work done, which is why the majority of the global population is sitting in chairs way too much.

So, how to avoid the almost inevitable chair-induced injury? One study authored by Dr. Waseem Amir Bashir of The University of Alberta Hospital, used an MRI to measure the spinal disk movement of three groups of people: one sitting, one slouching, and one reclining back at a 135-degree angle with their feet slightly elevated. The last group showed by far the least disk movement. So, short of bringing an exercise ball to work to keep your core engaged (which would, technically, help), the best option is to recline your chair almost as far as it will go, pull yourself closer to your workstation, and place your feet on a low object such as a step stool to keep your legs fairly straight. Just consider telling your boss first, so it doesn't look like you're trying to nap on the job!

# SOCIAL
# AND FUN

# Tweeting and Facebook Updating

## Oversharing—not just emotionally, but your physical location

You've seen the cringe-worthy Facebook update or Tweet—a diatribe against a recent ex with *way* too much personal information, especially about body part size. The complaint of a teen, with a hilarious repost by a parent or teacher. The emo, vague "sometimes it just isn't worth it" post, awkwardly begging for attention, and maybe followed by some cheesy song lyrics. You'd never do anything so embarrassing. But you're probably guilty of an entirely different overshare—disclosing your location, or allowing a friend to do so via check ins or even just innocent comments.

## Don't put it *all* out there

Be careful to avoid disclosing your location on social media. If you'd like to share where you had a really great dinner, make it in the past tense, not the present, when you're back home. If you're fortunate enough to not be one of the 3.4 million people who identified themselves as having a stalker, according to a United States Department of Justice Bureau's 2005–2006 survey (and that was just one year!), you still need to be vigilant against identity theft and robbery. And of people who did have a stalker, only about 10 percent (women) to 35 percent (men) were stalked by a stranger . . . so it's not that your Twitter followers or even your friends list *might* be harboring a quietly unstable person, it is an actual, real-world possibility.

The FBI hasn't yet released any data on the correlation between crimes and their social media connections, but cases have been documented on burglaries committed by someone on the victim's friends list. The first famous case was in spring of 2010, when Keri McMullen and Kurt Pendleton of New Albany, Indiana, shared via Facebook that they were going to an 8:00 P.M. concert; their house was burglarized at 8:42 P.M. Because they were selling the house and something had been broken in a showing, they had installed security cameras inside. Reviewing the footage of the theft clearly showed the face of someone on McMullen's friends list—someone she hadn't seen in twenty years, but had known since she was seven.

Shortly after that case, a Knoxville, Tennessee couple, Claudette and Boris McCubbin did what many happy couples on vacation do—posted all about it on Facebook. When they came back from their Florida vacation, they found their house robbed and ransacked, in such disarray they couldn't even get in the door. The perpetrator? Yes, a "friend" from their Facebook friends list.

Also in 2010, three New England men were arrested by New Hampshire's Nashua police for using social media to target eighteen robberies. Nashua Police Lt. Jeffrey Bukunt told David Lohr of AOL News: "In some of the cases, the residents or the residents' teenage children had put on Facebook and other sites that they [were] either away on vacation or out of town."

Still, the media attention from these and other cases (several involving celebrities) has done nothing to slow down the amount of "check ins" at a specific location, at a specific time via Foursquare, which can also be reposted to Twitter, and your friends can also check in/tag you in locations on Facebook, unless you specifically set your privacy settings so they can't.

The website *http://PleaseRobMe.com* highlights the safety problems of social media by posting information gathered from Twitter and Foursquare about vacant homes. The point of the site is not to attract or assist thieves, but to make people aware of the dangers of their posts.

Fox News and MSNBC had reports with similar tips about social media safety. The key points are:

- Privacy settings—use them to enable only friends to see your status updates and pictures.
- Vagueness is key—don't be specific in posting your whereabouts, or the times when you won't be in your home.
- With a little help from your friends—be sure to ask your friends not to share your information or whereabouts in *their* status updates.
- Your friends should be your friends—or at least acquaintances. Never add people you don't know.
- Protect your personal details—things like year of birth and place of birth can be used for identity theft.
- Vacation wisely—post pictures and details only after you've returned.
- Don't link your Facebook to your Twitter, if you'd like to keep your Twitter public. Otherwise it will automatically share your semiprivate Facebook updates onto your public Twitter feed.

- Stop allowing applications—a quiz created by the American Civil Liberties Union found quizzes allow an outside party to view your information, and in some cases, your friends' information.

The U.K. firm Credit Sesame sponsored a poll in 2010 of ex-burglars (in the United Kingdom only) and found that four out of five used social media to help them target empty homes. Daytime was almost twice as likely as nighttime for a home invasion to take place, so even posting something about your office can be dangerous. Make lists to filter such information to your *real* friends, or just share that information the old-fashioned way—in the real world.

# Having Difficult Conversations

## Thinking there's a winner or loser, or minimizing and smoothing over too quickly

People handle difficult conversations differently, but the majority is on either side of a spectrum. Some go into verbal battle with the gusto of a Mongol warrior, laying waste to all in their paths (even the innocent). On the other side of the spectrum, some have learned if they can't say anything nice, don't say anything at all. They hold back anything negative as much as possible, and when they absolutely must speak up, they are very careful in their tone and word choices to minimize the amount of negativity or criticism they use. One method is "strong" and one method is "nice," but they are both doing it wrong.

## Keep your eye off the prize

First, be aware of the preconceived notions of communication you've grown up with and accepted. In *Surviving Dreaded Conversations*, author Donna Flagg points out that "life simply has not provided us with sufficient opportunities to practice telling people things that they do not want to hear." Flagg then reminds us that, hey, opportunities *are* there, but society has decided lies are less destructive than the truth.

If you're an avoider, you might also be a minimizer. In *Failure to Communicate*, Holly Weeks points out that if a conversation *wasn't* complex, you wouldn't be feeling daunted to talk about it. To minimize your feelings is doing them a disservice, as sacrificing them to avoid an argument negates attempting the difficult conversation in the first place. Don't try to roll several problems into one in order to have only one conversation—each problem needs to be addressed on its own.

Weeks sees two opposite ends of the spectrum emerge as these conversations take place: confrontation and smoothing over. She advises that you aim for the middle of that range, and stay focused on your outcome, not "winning" or ending the conversation. When you get combative *or* minimize, neither of you is communicating what you actually need to, and thus ensure a failure.

That's right, aggressive types: Winning a difficult conversation isn't actually winning. Weeks's crucial advice is to avoid a "combat mentality," which is a default setting for many people when a conversation invokes unpleasant feelings such as anger, shame, or embarrassment. It's easier to lash out than to . . . gasp . . . process feelings. Especially in a work environment, but there especially, both conversation "winners" and "losers" tend to look like losers.

Both people involved in the conversation are likely to fall into using ploys such as lying, crying, threatening, or silence. If you're the one doing this, duh, stop it. It's a natural reaction, but it's not going to get anything accomplished. If someone takes this tactic with you, Weeks's solution is to address it directly. Be fair, and make sure you're letting the person respond, and not dismissing any legit information. Both sides should be allowed to take some time, if needed, to process or cool off. If someone's confrontation makes you feel ill, it's okay to ask for a few minutes to walk off those fight-or-flight chemicals. "Walk it off" isn't just for sports.

Another reason to avoid combat mentality is that a difficult conversation is likely to actually help someone. Flagg makes the analogy of how grateful we are when a friend points out we have spinach stuck in our teeth. "They don't let us walk around and embarrass ourselves," she says. "It's the same mindset, the same thing."

Whether you just had the salad or you need to point out something a little bigger than spinach, remember: Stay in the elusive middle ground between aggression and avoidance no matter what gets thrown, and keep your end goal in mind. You'll probably be surprised at how productive the (albeit unpleasant) conversation ends up being.

# Watching 3D Movies

## 3D causes eye strain

A new, big-budget film is out, with tons of action and special effects. You want the best seat in the house, the most buttery popcorn, and to get lost in the story for a while. The best way? Obviously that 3D ticket, so you feel right in the action. With everything popping up around you, you're bound to have a better experience, right? It seems like an obvious "yes," but professionals are telling us "no" and "no way."

## Stick to the old-fashioned way

If you have an option, just get a ticket to the 2D showing instead. A 2011 study from California State University found that viewers did not have increased enjoyment of a film viewed in 3D over one in 2D. Additionally, the researchers found viewers of 3D were more likely to experience eye strain and headaches.

As professor and optometrist Martin Banks explains it, "You're taking a normal relationship that has been coupled in the brain for years and you're changing that; we showed that can cause fatigue." He's referring to how the eyes converge when looking at objects close up and diverge when looking at objects far away, and how 3D requires the eyes to converge on one image and focus, leaving the eye oscillating between its natural inclination to focus on the whole screen, and the object coming toward them.

Northwest University ophthalmology professor Michael Rosenberg told Reuters's Julie Steenhuysen, "There are a lot of people walking around with minor eye problems . . . which . . . the brain deals with naturally." However, Rosenberg goes on to say that in a 3D film, people who previously did not realize they may have a vision problem will experience headaches and eye strain. In more extreme cases, some people have experienced motion sickness, nausea, dizziness, and fainting.

Headaches and nausea were probably the reason 3D never really got past the fad stage throughout its history, according to Rick Heineman, spokeperson for RealD, the provider of 3D equipment to most theaters in the United States. Heineman says that the older technology used two projectors, one for the right eye and one for the left. If the projectors were not set up properly, it would cause discomfort for many viewers. Today, a single digital projector switches between the left eye and right eye images 144 times *per second*. It's a huge improvement, but it doesn't change the fact it asks our eyes to focus in an unusual way that easily creates fatigue.

But for those who don't have a physical response to 3D, this research is still significant, as the study found that not only does 3D *not* enhance enjoyment, but viewers who watched a film in 3D were less likely to remember details about the film than filmgoers who watched a 2D version.

Oscar-winning, textbook-writing, sound designer, and film editor Walter Murch penned a letter to 3D humbug Roger Ebert, giving some insight on why 3D fails filmgoers on an emotional level:

"3D films remind the audience that they are in a certain 'perspective' relationship to the image," Murch wrote. "Whereas if the film story has really gripped an audience they are 'in' the picture in a kind of dreamlike 'spaceless' space."

Additionally, Murch points out the technical problems from his side. Because the eye needs more time to process the 3D image, 3D edits can never move as quickly as with a 2D film. Murch also discusses the problems of how the eye focuses on 3D, and how human eyes have never evolved to work in the way 3D requires, thus the end result can be "alienating."

"A good story will give you more dimensionality than you can ever cope with," Murch writes, and Ebert agrees. But if you're not likely to get a headache, are just looking for a fun visual, and don't want to give up 3D movies, film geeks would suggest you look for movies like *Avatar* that were shot with 3D cameras (called "native 3D"), rather than films shot in 2D and quickly converted to 3D to try to rake in more cash. It's a debatable difference. Some films, such as James Cameron's *Titanic,* have been converted to 3D with time and care, and the viewer will have a much better image than is the case with films that are quickly converted, like 2010's *Clash of the Titans*, which was only made 3D after *Avatar*'s success started a craze.

# Getting Revenge

## You only *think* it will make you feel better

Sweet or served cold, you've probably fantasized about or even exacted revenge at some time. Although the experience of desiring revenge runs the full gambit from sweeping social injustices to individual trauma, it pops up frequently for everyone on the small scale as well—aimed at another driver who cut you off in traffic, or the ex who broke your heart. People buy joke voodoo dolls in innocuous mall stores, write nasty things shamelessly on social media, and can even hire a delivery service to deliver a smelly dead fish or dead flowers.

As children, most of us read fairy tales based almost entirely in revenge. Even the slightly more modern and properly British *Peter Rabbit* is the story of a young rabbit finding self-actualization by avenging his father's death at the hands of an annoyed and hungry farmer. In school, we study endless literature and philosophy ruminating on revenge, and watch TV shows and films entirely based on the premise. Our histories are steeped in the concept, and statistically, almost everyone thinks revenge would make them feel better about a slight. The problem is, what we think we would feel and what we really feel when in a situation are two different issues. As it turns out scientifically, revenge doesn't actually "work" to make a victim feel better.

## HOW TO DO IT RIGHT
## Don't do it

Turns out poet George Herbert in the early 1600s was spot-on with his suggestion "living well is the best revenge." The best way to exact revenge is . . . to not take it.

You probably don't believe it, and according to science, no one does, but that doesn't change its veracity. A 2008 study by Kevin Carlsmith (Colgate University), Daniel T. Gibert (Harvard University), and Timothy Wilson (University of Virginia) found that all participants believed revenge would make them feel better about a personal injustice. But in multiple studies, the researchers found the study subjects who were able to exact revenge in a situation consistently felt *worse* than those who were not given a chance at revenge.

The researchers who conducted the study explain this as being related to "the accuracy of affective forecasting," wherein we predict how we will feel in a certain situation. They found when it comes to revenge, people's perceptions of how they would feel taking revenge were universally positive, but when people actually took revenge more negative emotional consequences resulted. Researchers found this to be true even in cases of substitution (which was recommended by psychologists for many years), such as hitting a punching bag or a pillow to release the pressure of wanting revenge. It's an idea commonly accepted since the time of Freud. But in 2002 a study by B. J. Bushman found that when study subjects were insulted and then given the chance at "cathartic aggression" via a punching bag, they remained more angry and longing for revenge than those who were insulted but given no options.

Bushman and colleagues, in another study in 2001, found the degree of revenge matched the degree of negative "affective consequences" to the revenge-seeker. In other words, the more serious the revenge, the worse the revenge-seeker felt afterwards, and the longer he or she held on to the pain of the original offense.

People firmly believed that taking their aggression out in other ways would bring healing, Carlsmith, Wilson, and Gilbert found, but their beliefs didn't translate into reality. "In sum," they wrote, "research shows that cathartic venting does not reduce subsequent aggression against the offending object."

The idea of "mood repair" is often discussed when it comes to revenge. Doctors Cathy Malchiodi and Regina Barreca wrote in *Psychology Today* about healing and the desire for revenge. Barreca cited a female CEO of a *Fortune* 500 company, who publicized a sexist employer's misogynistic pay records. The CEO told Barreca, "The best form of revenge is simply to let the truth be known."

Malchiodi acknowledges that truth can be healing, but not all situations lend themselves to truth-telling. With her patients in such cases, she relies on art therapy to help people create and reclaim their self-worth. She advises patients to write themselves the apology letters they wish to receive from their offenders. Malchiodi feels the desire to "get even" is actually a desire to "get whole again." She writes in *Psychology Today*: "we all have the possibility to recover whatever was lost, stolen, violated, disrespected or betrayed from those who hurt us which is the ultimate form of 'getting even.' "

The conclusion we can draw from all of this research? Revenge often causes the exact opposite of the desired outcome. Even though some people had the pleasure center of their brains briefly light up when exacting revenge, it wasn't "worth it"—they remained more upset, for longer periods, than those who did not take revenge. Acts of revenge seem to keep the wound fresh, and hold the offender in the revenger's mind. Looks like there's some truth to the old living well saying.

# Winning

## Overestimating the happiness produced by the achievement of winning, which might be an inferior learning experience to losing anyway

We all have variations in our levels of competitiveness, but chances are, you dream of winning. It probably started as a kid, playing sports. You wanted the trophy, the glory, the picture in the paper, and the praise. You imagined, with the insanely colorful imagination of a child, how good it would feel to win. And whether you won or lost, you carried that ideal with you into adulthood. Now you dream of winning in your career, winning the lottery, or your favorite football team winning the Superbowl. Maybe you even tried to win on a reality show, in a marathon, or on a softball league . . . or imagined that you did. You can imagine how perfect your life would be if Simon Cowell told you your voice was "brilliant" or you had a few million in cash in your hands.

The problem is twofold. Number one, valuable lessons are learned through losing—some psychologists argue these are *crucial* lessons. Number two, people tend to over-predict how they will feel in a hypothetical situation that hasn't yet unfolded. If you've tied all your hopes of happiness to one specific victory-to-be, it's time to reassess.

Remember when Vince Lombardi said, "Winning isn't everything, it's the only thing"? He also said he wished he'd never said that.

## HOW TO DO IT RIGHT
## Be the smart loser

Smile, say thank you, be humble, be grateful, acknowledge your competitors graciously. But you already knew that part. The real way to win "right" is to keep it in context of what it truly is. A win is not you. Your talent, or one specific measure of it, is not the sum of your worth. What we perceive as loss and failure motivates us to improve and grow. Let's not name any names, but just look at certain people born with silver spoons in their mouths who seem a bit . . . vapid, unmotivated, and ungrateful. Not anyone you'd want to hang out with, work with, or trust to date your kids someday. Those are people who were protected from "losing" and having to work hard to get better.

Dr. Tamar Chansky, author of *Freeing Your Child from Negative Thinking*, told Leslie Goldman with *Newsweek*, "It is going to feel bad to lose—at first—but it's just part of playing the game and everyone goes through it. The big picture is the way we improve at anything, is by trying, by working at it."

As cheesy as it sounds, your perception of winning could still be influenced by those days in Little League, with overbearing fathers, coaches, or gym teachers. According to Chansky, young children don't even have an understanding of what winning or losing really means, and generally aren't ready to start being scored until age ten. University of Colorado sociology professor Jay Coakley, PhD told *Newsweek* "in some cases we've foisted competitive rewards structures on our kids before they've learned to cooperate, and cooperation is the foundation of ethical competition."

You've probably run into someone who missed that "ethical competition" lesson at a key time in his development, and has brought that missing chip into adulthood. This is where Lombardi regretted his famous quote, saying, "I meant the effort. I meant having a goal. I sure didn't mean for people to crush human values and morality."

Releasing the notions others have imposed on us about winning is an important step to keeping a victory in its proper context. Another step is to keep *yourself* in context outside of the competition. Jennifer Hamady is a singer and author of *The Art of Singing*, which highlights the psychology of self-expression. Hamady was also a back-up singer on *American Idol*, and found herself advising the contestants. Her most important words were also the hardest for the contestants to grasp: "You are not your talent."

"Your specialness has nothing to do with what you do," she told them. "It is an internal quality—an inherent gift—that is yours forever, whether or not you ever sing another note." Hamady notes the young singers frequently weren't able to believe or fully understand this concept. She remarks on society's insistence of not differentiating the talent from the person. "As a result," she wrote in *Psychology Today*, "we tend to celebrate people for what they do, not for who they are, reinforcing the notion that 'it' is more important—and more valuable—than them."

Once you redefine the importance of winning and separate yourself (and self-worth) from a particular victory, there's one more little issue—we're unable to accurately predict how winning would feel to us, and tend to overestimate it. Social scientist Daniel Gilbert, author of *Stumbling on Happiness*, has done extensive studies on happiness, and found people are poor predictors of how bad or how good a situation will make them feel. He gave *Smithsonian* magazine the example of winning the lottery. It doesn't matter how often we see reports of various lottery winners unhappy years after the event, we still think our experience would be different. The reason a win doesn't bring lasting happiness, he says, is, "We're resilient in both directions. We rebound from distress but we also rebound from joy."

All of this doesn't mean it's not awesome to win. Usually, it is. But don't let winning run your life or define you. Don't be afraid to lose (and learn) and be sure to keep the importance of victory in the context of reality.

# Sharing Your Goals

## Sharing your goals

You just got a hot new idea, and you know it's going to take a lot of work to achieve, but whatever, you're fired up about it. You call a friend, a parent, a sibling, or maybe even just chat idly with a neighbor, and you can't wait to tell them what you intend to do. This is an especially great idea for a difficult goal, because it really holds you to the fire, right? Now that someone knows, that person will have an *expectation* of your achievement, so you can't just get distracted by another goal and forget all about this one, because that person will *ask you* about it later! Now that you've told someone, you have to "keep your word" and "put your money where your mouth is."

The logic is there, but it turns out, that's the opposite of how it actually ends up working.

## Keep it to yourself

Write your goals down instead of sharing them. Or, if you really have to share, acknowledge the negative, such as "I really want to learn Japanese, but I have a long way to go and it's not going to be easy." Something strange happens in our brains when we present a goal in the positive, as a "satisfaction"—the positive response we get gives us a sense of "reward" as if *we'd already accomplished the goal.*

People started getting wise to this idea back in the 1930s, when Wera Mahler and G. H. Mead published separate studies about the nature of how we define ourselves. Mead found that people define themselves based on a skill, such as "athlete," "guitarist," or "parent." We set goals that further define ourselves, and these goals require "social recognition." Mahler found that when given a task, we have set in place a "tension system," which doesn't let up until the task is completed. Mahler found that if a goal was interrupted by introducing a new goal, the new tension system would take focus from the old tension system, and the original goal was far less likely to be completed.

The problem with sharing your goal verbally in the positive is that receiving the positive feedback seems to ease the tension system, as if you'd already accomplished the goal. And just like Mahler's subjects, once the tension is shifted, the original goal is less likely to ever be completed. Mahler also found acknowledgment of a goal made it feel like a reality in the subject's brain.

Robert A. Wicklund and Peter M. Gollwitzer expanded these ideas in the 1980s in "Symbolic Self-Completion, Attempted Influence, and Self-Deprecation," which has a pretty self-explanatory title. But they left out the part about "speaking of your goals tells your brain they're a social reality," because that's exactly what they found. It seems the symbols of our identity that we earn through goals can actually be created just by our words of the goals, instead of actual action. Gollwitzer took it further with tests, and later published "When Intentions Go Public: Does Social Reality Widen the Intention-Behavior Gap?" The take-away, in fancy science-speak, translates to, "share your goals and you're less likely to complete them."

Put any study under a microscope and it's easy to pick apart, so the cool thing about Gollwitzer's findings is they involved multiple studies by multiple scientists over about an eighty-year period.

One of Gollwitzer's tests required his subjects to write down their goals. Half of them shared their goals out loud, and half of them kept their goals to themselves. They were then given forty-five minutes of goal-related work. Those who had not shared their goals worked the whole time, after which they said they felt frustrated with the huge amount of work they still had to do to achieve their goals. The goal-sharers, however, quit before their time was up, and said they felt optimistic about being closer to their goals. Sure, optimism is great, but which group *actually* got closer to achievement?

# Giving and Receiving Compliments

HOW YOU'RE DOING IT WRONG

Saying something to dismiss a compliment may seem humble, but you probably just insulted your compliment-giver. When giving compliments, keep in mind differences in perception.

A beautiful woman in her early thirties, Jen has a hard time taking compliments. She explains that she was always taught saying "thank you" to a compliment was akin to saying "I know," and is rude—and she's not alone. Men and women shake off compliments about appearance, work performance, or even their clothing. However, by dismissing someone's heartfelt kind words, you just created an awkward situation . . . or caused her to repeat the compliment, with some rephrasing . . . or made him look stupid around the ten other people at the party who interpreted your response as putting the *dis* in "dismissing" the compliment-giver.

Okay, so you know to say "thank you." But said with the wrong tone or look, it's easy for someone to feel that "thank you" might really mean *%@! you. So, how *do* you accept a compliment?

## HOW TO DO IT RIGHT

# Show your gratitude

If you shouldn't ignore it, or say "it's nothing," and you shouldn't *just* say "thank you," how are you supposed to take a compliment? First, say thank you, just don't *only* say thank you and stay stone-faced. As psycho-therapist Dr. Simon Feuerman points out, people who are enraged or anxious may swing into a form of "grat-itude"; thus, a tight-lipped "thank you" from a per-son who's anxious with anger may easily be confused with a tight-lipped "thank you" from someone anx-ious about receiving praise. Follow up the thank you with a related comment such as "glad you enjoyed it," or "thanks for recognizing the effort, I worked really hard." If you don't have anything else to say, a *sincere* smile is as good as any words. "It's almost like a dance," says University of Cincinnati communication profes-sor LisaMarie Luccioni, "your partner initiates (com-pliment) and you respond (expression of gratitude)."

If you take the old-school approach, feeling that acknowledging a compliment is immodest or arrogant, bear in mind the compliment-giver may not feel the same way, and might find your lack of response awk-ward, alienating, or downright insulting.

When taking a compliment, be aware of your body language. Discomfort with taking compliments may cause you to cross your arms—which even dogs know isn't the body language of a receptive person, and no, they can't have your bacon. A slight lean forward and eye contact will help communicate that you accept the compliment (and here pup, have some bacon).

"Fight the urge to downplay the compliment," advises Luccioni, as that "may be read as a personal rejection." Luccioni also recommended against the common impulse to "one-up" the compliment, by trying to lavish an even better compliment on the original giver.

When giving compliments, if you're not sincere, it can be perceived as antagonistic.

When giving and receiving compliments, men and women tend to do it differently, although both are guilty of defaulting to appearance-related compliments. A woman complimenting a man is more likely to prefer to do so without others present, and may be more likely to give a compliment a man finds out of context. In *Men's Health*, Shefalee Vasudev uses the analogy of a man giving a business presentation who finds himself complimented on his shoes. Here the subject of the compliment may be confused, or even suspicious, even though the giver of the compliment is sincere.

These differences are certainly not limited to only gender. If you are suspicious of the sincerity of a compliment, try not to immediately react negatively. Try to assess the situation: what is said, who is saying it, and what the person's goal might be. The best way to handle it either way is with grace. Author and teacher Dustin Wax points out that if you assume a person didn't mean a compliment, "responding as if they did disarms whatever ulterior motive they might have."

Compliment through teasing? Don't be surprised if someone gets upset with you, you insensitive ass. Psychologists have observed men are more likely to "play fight" as a way of giving a compliment, and women are more likely to be offended and not realize the intent was actually a compliment.

The best way to play it safe? Give—and accept—compliments sincerely.

# Speaking

## Your everyday speaking voice is probably suffering from one of these very common maladies

You're not going to be announcing for *Monday Night Football* anytime soon, so who cares if you've never paid any attention to your speaking voice? In fact, you avoid it—you dislike hearing your outgoing voicemail message, or hearing yourself on your friends' voicemails if played back to you. But it is what it is, nothing to be done about it now. And again, who cares—you're not doing any public speaking!

## Avoid the vocal fry

Relax, breathe, and give your cell phone a break. Our voices are shaped by our physical structures as well as our habits, and most of us have some pretty bad habits.

The muscles and cartilage affecting your voice are molded by the vocal habits of a lifetime, and practicing new techniques creates new molding. So why should you care? Because people are judging you, that's why. And you're way too cool to care. But Dr. Kenneth Crannell points out that our voices are a representation of ourselves, and thus if we create a voice of excellence, we are more likely to feel excellent as well, besides projecting said excellence to others.

The most recent trend in vocal wrongness is called "vocal fry." Vocal fry is created when someone slips into a lower tone, usually at the end of a sentence, and this tone has a "fried" or "creaky" quality. Britney Spears and Kim Kardashian are infamous for this way of speaking, but research indicates men tend to speak with this raspy flaw as well. And vocal fry is on the rise, with two-thirds of college students in one study displaying it. The problem with using it is it conveys a sense that you're not confident, or in some cases, sure of what you are saying.

Vocal fry is caused by tension and improper breathing. Stress or excitement adds to vocal fry, and often the speaker has simply run out of air. Dr. Crannell suggests breathing exercises to improve diaphragmatic breathing. By lying down and placing a book on your abdomen, you can see how the book lifts with each breath—it should move evenly on your inhalation. Step up the exercise by sitting up with your legs bent, and slowly lowering yourself back to the floor, to allow you to feel your rectus abdominus muscle.

You can then practice using uncontrolled versus controlled breathing. For uncontrolled, take a deep, diaphragmatic breath and read two lines of poetry as the breath slowly escapes out of you "like a punctured balloon," Crannell says. For the controlled breath, read the same two lines of poetry after a deep, diaphragmatic breath, but this time use the air in a controlled way, to try to fill the room with your voice. Use the tension in your abdomen that you felt when doing that reverse sit-up before—*not* tension in your throat, mouth, or sinus area. You should begin to feel the differences possible with breath control.

Another common speech mistake is glottal shock, which is caused by breath escaping unevenly due to tension in the vocal folds. Author G. Robert Jacks describes it as "that sort of sharp, staccato, cough-like click in which I produce a word starting with a vowel sound." Jacks describes the cause as vocal bands being "blasted apart by breath pressure." You feel this right before you cough, and you may be unaware of doing it while speaking. To feel the difference, practice pronouncing words that begin with vowels with an "h" in front of the word, for example "also" becomes "halso"—you'll feel your throat open.

To protect your vocal cords, the American Academy of Otolaryngology advises against excessive speaking in loud places, using too high or too low a pitch, and—big surprise—avoiding excessive cell phone chatting. Now who wants to tell Kim and Britney to hang up their phones and breathe?

# Taking Pictures

## HOW YOU'RE DOING IT WRONG

### You're overusing the rule of thirds, and "Myspace angles" are so 2004

Time to snap a few photos of yourself and your friends. You hold the camera up at an angle and aim it at yourself. Then you take a picture of your friend, perfectly centering her face in the frame. You remember high school art class, with the rule of thirds, which divides the image into a three-by-three grid like the end of *The Brady Bunch* opener, with the subject being your "Alice" in the middle square.

## HOW TO DO IT RIGHT

### Avoid the middle

Forget about centering, but also stop going for the crazy angles. To address the rule of thirds, George Field shot down the idea (a bit) in his classic 1845 book *Chromatics*, saying, "This rule . . . would produce a uniform and monotonous practice."

Raluca Chase of Kalura Photography puts it in more modern words, saying to nonprofessional picture-snappers "the eye needs to look a little bit for the subject, in order to make the picture interesting—if it's in the middle it (the eye) just moves on to the next picture."

Documentary photographer Philip Martin of Los Angeles agrees with Chase. "No more floating heads," Martin suggests, saying many nonprofessionals "center the subject's head in the frame, even if it's a portrait-oriented photo. There's nothing to establish where the subject is." The kind of "floating head portraits" Martin advises against are fairly common on social networking sites, where someone will post a picture in which her in-focus head is in the "Alice" space in the rule-of-thirds center, with the off-focus background taking up the majority of the picture (the other eight imaginary squares).

Social media is a huge part of why photography has a growing importance among nonprofessionals. Access to technology such as digital cameras and photo-editing software has opened what was once professional-only to the public, but the public doesn't always take the time to do it right.

Jessica Bettcher of Jessica Bettcher Photography and Bettcher Design has a unique perspective. As the art director and producer of the Lady Luck Burlesque troupe, Bettcher's eye has developed to appreciate the old school. Bettcher says she could reminisce all day "about the beautiful days of film and knowing that you got it right, not hoping that you did." What she sees often in nonprofessional photography is a complete reliance on the automatic flash, and tons of washed-out, red-eyed pictures as a result. Bettcher says "taking the time to understand the value of changing the aperture" would only take a "quick study" and would bring huge improvement to most people's photos. "Folks rely too heavily on Photoshop to 'fix' a photo rather than strive to take a good one in the first place," she says.

And speaking of your personal access to technology, if you haven't already, go ahead and stop with the crazy angles, also known as "Myspace angles" due to their prominence on the social networking site—yes, those angles are right up there with "duck lips" in the doing-it-wrong of self portraits! (Men do "duck lips" too, but it looks more like a sneer.) Chase, in her dry, direct Eastern European way of speaking, says "No more tilting of cameras—if I have to turn my neck in order to understand a photo, then there is a problem with it." In other words, you're doing it wrong.

Sadly, if you are a female on a dating site, statistically, a "Myspace angle" picture *will* work for you, no matter how many times the potential suitors viewing your picture have seen this to be deceptive. But for *any* other occasion, the world has caught on to the angles and feels like you're trying too hard, so knock it off.

# Talking on Your Cell Phone

## You can't actually hear yourself on your cell, so you probably don't realize you, yes *you*, are one of those annoying talkers

Of course *you* don't chat on your cell phone in public. You'd never be so classless. Now you'd better stop, drop, and roll, cause your pants are on fire. If you've ever made a call within earshot of another person, and you're not a speech or audio expert, you were definitely way too loud. Feedback, also called "sidetone," on cell phones causes *everyone* to shout, because your ear can't hear itself to adjust your volume. (To experiment with this, try talking with earplugs in. You're probably going to have excessive volume.)

In a poll by *Microsoft.com*, loud conversation in public was the top cell etiquette offender for 72 percent of Americans. So if it's cool to have 72 percent of people giving you the stink eye, judging your conversation—and evaluating how punchable your face is—by all means, keep chatting.

## HOW TO DO IT RIGHT

## Know Thyself's Volume

You need to be aware of your volume when using cell phones. Even in your own home—if you share it with others, or live in an apartment—you're probably annoying someone.

First of all, duh, unless it's an emergency, never talk on your cell in an enclosed space, like a subway car, coffee shop, waiting room, or even a store, where your voice is just bouncing off the walls. Larry Magid, a technology analyst with *CBS News*, likens the public cell conversation with public smoking. He advises to keep the phone on vibrate when you're with other people, and if you need to take a call, excuse yourself and step into a private area. Magid points out that Amtrak used to have smoking cars, and now have "quiet cars" where passengers are free from listening to the yap of cell talkers. If it's a place you shouldn't be smoking, you're being gauche to have a nonemergency conversation as well. In the future, it may well be taken just as seriously as smoking—in 2011, an Ohio woman was arrested and removed from an Amtrak train's quiet car after ignoring multiple requests (for hours) that she stop jabbering away on her cell.

When you do talk on a cell phone, be conscious of your volume. Like earplugs, sidetone doesn't allow you to hear your own volume, so you are *not aware* you're being too loud. If Helen Keller learned how to talk, you can figure it out with your cell. You might feel ridiculous (and you are, but to a good end), but go ahead and experiment with your volume, so you know what it feels like when your volume isn't raised or hushed, but at a happy medium. You will need to know the proper volume of your voice by feel, because thanks to sidetone, you won't be able to hear it.

Coauthor of *Annoying: The Science of What Bugs Us*, Flora Lichtman says, "It's not just about the sound intruding your space. It seems to be about the speech itself." Lichtman's test subjects consistently found hearing half a conversation extremely annoying, even when cell phones and volume weren't factors. The annoyance factor is nothing new—in fact Mark Twain wrote an essay on the annoyance of hearing half a conversation via telephone a mere four years after the phone's debut. And you *know* you don't wanna be steppin' on Twain.

The remedy for this is often very simple: Just step away if you must talk. In your home, or anywhere that's not like the North Pole in human habitation, moderate your volume.

New York City restaurateur Danny Meyer is one of many who have banned cell phone use inside their eateries. *New York Times* columnist Randy Cohen ("The Ethicist") explained, "There are different expectations at McDonald's than at a fancy restaurant. Courtesy, however, is not reserved for the wealthy."

Proper etiquette and common courtesy also dictate you should avoid talking while interacting with sales clerks or any other humans. You may have noticed some signs in shops saying "we will be happy to assist you when you're not on your phone," which of course is polite longhand for STFU.

So step aside, excuse yourself, and be aware of your volume. Mark Twain's ghost and 72 percent of the population will thank you for it . . . yes, even people who live with you, or the neighbors you share a wall with will thank you.

# Traveling Internationally

## Be a traveler, not a tourist

It's about time you finally kicked back and took a vacation, so when you see an ad for a deep discount cruise or all-inclusive resort, you jump at it. This is going to be so great: all the food, shopping, and fun you can cram into a foreign country. You can't wait to get there and . . . not leave the resort grounds?

## Stretch your limits

Dig a little harder to find an adventure. You may have to spend a little more than for an all-inclusive resort package, but it will be well worth it when you feel like you actually left the country, rather than spending all your time on a beach that might as well have been in Florida. A little more work will earn you the title of "traveler" instead of "tourist."

Bruce Poon Tip is at the forefront of the traveler scene with his company, G Adventures, formerly known as GAP Adventures, which stood for Great Adventure People. Poon Tip has been so successful with these adventures that he and his company have been loaded with awards, such as National Geographic

Adventures naming them "the best 'Do It All Outfitter' on Earth."

Poon Tip's focus is sustainable travel, which many find to be the best kind of travel, as it is a more rewarding experience to interact with the people in a new country. Poon Tip explains why sustainable travel is a superior way to go: "In the past, the consumer is just on a quest for their vacation. In the sustainable model, everyone achieves happiness in the transaction—consumer, operator, and people on the ground who supply the service. Poon Tip's tips (how is that not a column?) on international travel come from an actual world of experience and include these shiny gems:

- Feel like you're traveling: pushing past the familiar is what leads to the most rewarding travel experience, with more learning opportunities and chances for personal growth, and more chances when you come home to appreciate what you've experienced—and what you get to come home to!
- The resort is not your travel advisor: but it will try to be. "The resorts are trained to keep you on the resort and spend your money there," Poon Tip warns. Resorts can often be very difficult to leave. Poon Tip likened his attempt to go off-property at one Caribbean resort to leaving the Death Star. If your resort makes you think of the Dark Side of the Force, everyone involved is doing it wrong! Safety is important, but resorts are also sometimes guilty of fear-mongering to keep people (and their money) on the property. Don't trust the resort for safety information—do the research yourself. Travel warnings are posted at *travel.state.gov* and utilize message boards to track down "insider info"

from around the globe. "The Thorn Tree" message boards at *lonelyplanet.com* are hugely popular, as well as the forums at *bootsnall.com*.

- Tear down the wall: when someone local is providing you with a service, it forms a sort of "politeness service wall" that can keep you at an arm's length. To truly experience a foreign culture, Poon Tip recommends sharing a meal with locals, if possible. Breaking bread together is a universal bonding experience, as food speaks every language. Music and families are good wall-busters too. Given a chance to participate in an anything musical—jump on it! It doesn't even matter if you suck; it's the effort that counts. And if you find yourself with the opportunity to strike up a conversation with a local, sharing pictures of your hometown and family (especially when staying in a guest house and seeing their home and family) is also a way to be socially warm.

- Keep it real: if getting up close and personal isn't your style, it's still easy to have a true cultural experience by shopping at the local venues and eating local food. This is different than what a resort provides—they make an effort of authenticity in the array of food and souvenirs they offer on their grounds, and they may even try to make it seem organic to the location, but if it's on resort property, it is all filtered by the company. It is not exactly a reflection of the culture, but how the hospitality execs decided they wanted the culture to feel to visitors. For the "real thing," break free from corporate property! Even if you are booked on a business trip and didn't get a choice in the resort, make the effort to get off the property at some point—even just a few hours could make a difference in your experience. Remember to do your own online research beforehand to pick out safe restaurants and neighborhoods nearby.

To make the most of your time off, make sure to go for an enriching, warm, empowering, adventurous experience. If you want to lounge around a restricted area, you don't need to leave the country!

# FOOD AND BEVERAGE

# Measuring Flour

## A cup holds more than a cup . . . or maybe less

Maybe you prefer the kind of cookie dough that comes in a tube. In fact, you're not even going to bake it, you're going to nom that dough raw. Stomachache be damned! But now as you're happily chowing down, you start casually reading the ingredients on the package, and suddenly you're just not that hungry anymore. What are those words? Is this cookie dough, or rocket fuel? You can do way better and make your own. It's simple! Eggs, flour, sugar . . . other stuff. You find a recipe, and dip your measuring cup in the flour, level it off like a pro, and dump it in the bowl. It was a perfect-*looking* cup, but you have too much flour now, because you don't even know you just did it wrong.

## Use a scale

Flour needs to be weighed, not scooped in a measuring cup. The problem with the tricky powder is that it can be light and fluffy, or clump. And light flour and packed flour fit in the same cup measure, but have different total masses. If a recipe asks for 3 cups of flour, there can be up to 6 ounces in variation inside that 3 cups—about a whole cup off!

If you know you are never, ever going to bother to invest in a scale no matter how many baked goods you ruin, one simple way to minimize how much you compact your flour is to stop scooping it out of the bag. Each scoop packs the flour tightly together, and you can even accidentally tamp it down further when you level off the cup. Use a spoon to fill the cup, and when you level off, do so lightly, so as not to apply any downward pressure.

Professional recipe tester Linda Larsen attests that she has often seen cooks measure flour wrong on TV shows. Larsen has published several cookbooks and worked in the test kitchen for five Pillsbury Bake-Offs, so we can take her word on it.

# Choosing Produce

## That item isn't as ripe or bad as you think it is

Grabbing a few basic fruits and veggies at the grocery store or farmers' market isn't exactly brain surgery, and no one has much patience for those people who repeatedly inspect, prod, and take the rectal temperature of every piece. You know you want bananas without any brown spots, some nice big carrots, some oranges with no splotches, and you'll probably want a lemon eventually, but not in the next couple days, so you'll just get the one that's still green. You're not a Rockefeller, so you can't buy all organic—you just get the organic bananas.

Don't worry, the overcautious shopper did it wrong too (even if only by being annoying).

## HOW TO DO IT RIGHT

## Know that beauty is only skin deep

You're right in the basics: no slime, mold, squishiness, or black spots. But in some cases, spots are just fine, and avoiding them may cause you to miss out on the fruit or veggie that's at its perfect ripeness.

- Bananas are actually at their tastiest when they have a few brown spots. These spots are of the "small dot" variety, *not* bruises. The sweetness of a banana depends on its perfect ripeness, as anyone who has bitten into a greenish and un-sweet banana can tell you. Unlike a bruise, those little brown dots *do not* mean that it's brown underneath—it means it's sweet and ready to be eaten!

- Carrots are one of the most nutritious veggies out there, so don't skip them! Fat slices of carrot might look good in your salad, but bigger carrots have tougher centers. Smaller, baby carrots are also sweeter if you prefer that flavor. Because carrots grow right in the ground, they are more vulnerable to synthetic pesticide residues than some other choices, so go organic on these. Of course, carrots with cracks, blemishes, and a rubbery feel when bent are to be avoided, but even nonorganic carrots that "look" good might be carrying more "ingredients" than you want to ingest.

- Oranges, lemons, and other citrus fruit can't usually be judged by their color. Color isn't reflective of citrus's ripeness, so don't worry about a few color splotches on your orange. Bruises and cuts are no good, but those little whitish, green, or brown-colored patches are fine so long as the fruit feels heavy, firm, and has smooth skin. Citrus ripens from the inside out, so you might accidentally select an overripe fruit if you're too picky avoiding all the ones with imperfect color. Citrus fruits *stop ripening* once they are picked; therefore, choosing a greener lemon so it will last longer just means you will have a less-ripe lemon . . . it won't ripen in your kitchen like bananas or apples do.

If you're not able to buy everything organic, choose your organic carefully. Fruits such as bananas and oranges with thick peels have some insulation against chemical residues. But in-ground veggies such as carrots and potatoes, and thin and edible-skinned fruits such as apples are where you want to splurge your extra money on organic to avoid some nasty stuff. There's no need to inspect every piece like a CSI agent—you can determine the best with a quick squeeze and an once-over, now that you know a few secrets.

# Homebrewing Beer

## In a word: sanitation

Delicious homebrew. Well, it's delicious if you like drinking hairspray. But not to worry, you've been reading up on all the tricks of the trade, and you know your first few batches won't be very good, and even the most devoted friend might not be able to humor you with a sip. You are studying these recipes like you're the Gordon freakin' Ramsay of beer, and it's just a matter of time until you will be chef of your own homebrew kitchen. Yup, pretty soon you'll be expanding out of that closet. You know it takes patience. Brewing takes time! It involves live organisms! It's an absolute art. You're even avoiding the typical rookie mistake of storing at the wrong temperature. Yup . . . you have done your homework with all these ingredients and methods.

But you didn't read the difference between cleaning and sanitizing?

## Bleach the s**t out of those microorganisms

Even brewers who clean their equipment (because there's plenty of slackers out there in the cleaning department) are making a mistake when they don't do so with bleach. There is a difference between cleaning and sanitizing. Your clean bottles, fermenter, and air lock might have been thoroughly washed and look great, but they can still harbor microorganisms that can ruin your homebrew. If you are scrubbing plastic parts, you're doing even more damage, as abrasive cleaning can create microscopic cracks for bacteria to invade. Cleaning removes all visible dirt; sanitizing removes most of the invisible organisms that could starve your yeast or cause other problems, like making you sick!

Marty Nachel, author of *Homebrewing for Dummies*, said of homebrewers: "I don't think enough of them take the sanitation seriously." You can buy a variety of commercial sanitizers, or if you don't have a ton of money to burn, just use 1 ounce of household bleach per gallon of water.

Wasn't there something about vinegar, too? First of all, *never* add vinegar to undiluted bleach! Vinegar helps so you don't need to rinse the bleach as much, risking recontamination with tap water. But vinegar added directly to bleach causes a toxic gas. And not a cough-cough toxic gas, a potentially *fatal* toxic gas. Got it? Potentially fatal. Just had to say it again.

Now that we've remembered safety first, add an equal amount of vinegar as you did bleach to your diluted bleach solution. The vinegar reduces the pH of the bleach and helps supercharge its microorganism-killing abilities. Charlie Talley from Five Star Chemicals recommends 1 ounce of bleach and 1 ounce of white vinegar per 5 gallons of water; first add the bleach to the water, mix, and then add the vinegar.

Make sure you thoroughly rinse off all your equipment after sanitizing. Leftover bleach residue can leave a taste like sore throat medicine, and can also kill off some of your yeast. The simple way to tell if everything is well rinsed is that there's no trace of bleach smell left.

Bleach can cause aluminum and even stainless steel to corrode, but you can find stainless steel cleaner in the supermarket, so keep the bleach away from these parts.

Homebrewing has only been legal since 1979, so while doing all that washing and sanitizing, don't forget to feel bad-ass.

# Choosing and Using Knives

## That fifty-piece set is about forty-five more knives than you need, and stop ruining them in the dishwasher, and stop chopping!

Probably sometime after you stopped living in your childhood home or dorm, you realized you had to get some knives. And lo and behold, a discount store had a ginormous set for forty bucks. Those are all the knives you'll ever need! You're pretty sure about knife safety, like chopping away from yourself and putting them in the dishwasher blade-down. You place all five fingers on the handle firmly and chop away. You're definitely not like those guys who leave reality cooking shows after a nasty knife mishap, pretending they're not crying. Bring the cameras on in, 'cause your fifty knives have just chopped the best green pepper ever. Put that on a frozen pizza and it's practically health food. *Bam!*

## Change everything you're doing

If you're not a chef, a culinary student, or a seriously wannabe culinary student, you only need three to five knives. Sorry to be the bearer of hand-washing news, but those small knives should never go in the dishwasher. And I know you think you're being safe and fancy, but all fingers don't go on the handle, and rocking is a superior technique to chopping.

Beginning with knife selection: That huge set of cheap knives is way more crap than you need, and you get what you pay for—it's not going to be a great product at that price. You don't have to spend $100 per knife, but you're better off just buying the most useful kinds of knives individually.

According to Norman Weinstein at the Institute of Culinary Education in New York, the most important knife to have is a chef's knife with a blade of 8 to 10 inches in length. The knife should feel well-balanced when you hold it, meaning neither the blade nor the handle feels heavier.

The second handiest knife is a 2- to 4-inch-blade paring knife for smaller tasks like peeling and cutting fruits and veggies (such as tomatoes), and removing dark veins from shrimp. Weinstein advises that your last essential knife is a good bread knife, which is serrated and basically works like a wood saw, and cuts bread, bagels, and any tomatoes too big for the paring knife. A proper chef may not advise it lest you dull your blade too quickly, but a good bread knife will slice almost any normal foodstuff, including meat and firm vegetables.

When you are using the knife, instead of holding the handle with all of your fingers, use your thumb and forefinger to pinch the blade, which will give you more control, and keep your arm relaxed. A chopping motion is too . . . choppy. The movements should be smooth; Weinstein compares it to golf or tennis. A rocking motion with the knife leads to smoother, quicker results than chopping. You can't learn knife skills by reading, but you can find free tutorial videos online. It will take a lot of practice to become proficient and comfortable with your knives.

Now that you've chosen and used your knives, keep them sharp with a honing steel. After using the knife, you need to slice both sides of it at a 22-degree angle. Don't be shy about asking to see the proper motion when you buy the steel. If you're stuck with a clerk who gives you a blank stare, once again, check online videos for a visual; once you know how, it's very simple. If you've sprung for really good knives, take them to a professional to be sharpened. No matter what an infomercial says, at-home sharpening just doesn't really work.

To keep your blades sharp, wash by hand and don't put them in the dishwasher. Dishwashing detergent is strong stuff, and combine that with the water and heat, and you get dull blades and warped handles. It may seem like a lot of work, but quick swipes across the honing steel and an almost equally quick hand wash will actually be *less* work than laboring with an inferior, dull knife.

# Roasting Vegetables

## HOW YOU'RE DOING IT WRONG

### Most people actually "bake" rather than roast, and end up with unbrowned, unevenly cooked, and not very tasty vegetables

You know you need to eat vegetables, and even if you hate cooking, you want some variety on raw or steamed. The easy solution? Roasting! You chop up some veggies, toss them in that easy-to-clean glass pan, and put them in the oven at about 350ºF. They don't taste very good when they come out, but they're vegetables—how good can they be?

## HOW TO DO IT RIGHT

### Turn up the heat

You must cook at 500°F to roast; lower temperatures are actually baking. A metal pan is the best choice, and you need to cut the vegetables properly.

You already read up on knives, so you know you cut them properly! But properly for roasting means making them fairly uniform in size so they will cook evenly. Denser vegetables, such as root vegetables, will cook slower, so cut them into smaller sections than the lighter veggies.

Lisa Jervis, author of *Cook Food*, has some great advice on how to save the world from soggy, gross vegetables. She points out that many people pile the vegetables into a glass pan, but glass doesn't conduct heat to the vegetables like metal does, so a metal pan is ideal to get some delicious browning. A pan with 1-inch sides lets the steam escape for your roasts to get crispy on the outside.

When you arrange the vegetables, don't just dump them in a pile . . . the jumble won't cook evenly, and the ones on the bottom get squishy and can't brown. Lay them out flat on the pan, and cover with enough olive oil (butter will burn at the roasting temperature, so don't use it) to see the shiny coating on them. Sprinkle with salt and your favorite seasonings. Put in the oven at 500ºF for about thirty to forty minutes. The browning may make the vegetables look burned, but if roasted properly they will be browned and crunchy on the outside, and soft on the inside.

Roasting vegetables is a good way to make them taste better, especially if you're someone who doesn't love vegetables and needs to get more in your diet. Some of the most nutritious vegetables also roast well. Sweet potatoes have fiber, potassium, vitamin C, and free-radical fighting carotenoids. Cut the dense potatoes a bit smaller than your broccoli—and you do want to include broccoli, because it's a super-food that also contains carotenoids and vitamin C, as well as vitamin K and folic acid. Also cut butternut squash into smaller cubes than your broccoli. It contains vitamins A and C, and fiber, and has a nice roasted flavor for the pickiest of palates.

You probably already know eating vegetables can lower your cancer and heart disease risk, but veggies just aren't the most popular food (unless you are a goat, in which case, how are you reading this?). So finding a tastier way to do a proper roast can encourage you to eat more of them, and be healthier, and give you some bragging rights next time you hear someone drone on about how they are "cleansing" but they don't know the right way to roast a carrot!

# Eating Sushi

## HOW YOU'RE DOING IT WRONG

### Using chopsticks and adding soy sauce and wasabi

Going to a sushi restaurant, you sit at a table and order a few rolls off the menu. When the food comes, you slather it with wasabi, soy sauce, and ginger, before putting your chopsticks into action and eating. Or you add a bit of wasabi to a small dish of soy sauce and dip your sushi in before eating, with help from your chopsticks. It might taste perfectly delicious to you, but everything you just did was totally wrong.

## HOW TO DO IT RIGHT

### Keep it simple

Sushi concierge and author of *The Story of Sushi*, Trevor Corson, has plenty of advice for the erroneous sushi lover. His first is to find a sushi bar, where you can speak to the chef and find out what the best fish is that day. Sushi rolls are actually a Westernization, evolving in form since the invention of the aptly named "California roll." Request *nigiri*—the chef will compact rectangles of fish and rice by hand. Nigiri may also include a bit of wasabi, and have a *neta* (topping) such as salmon or tuna.

Corson explains that "good sushi" falls apart when chopsticks are used. The traditional and proper way to eat sushi is with your fingers, bringing the nigiri straight from the small sushi dish into your mouth, where it should fall apart on your tongue.

As for those concoctions of soy sauce and wasabi you adore—it's actually a distraction from the taste of the fish. A sushi chef will season nigiri to his expert discretion, and hence, it goes straight from plate to mouth without second-guessing his seasoning mastery.

If the chef does not season the fish, dip a corner in soy sauce. And that ginger you pile on top of your fish? It's actually a "palate cleanser" *not* a seasoning. Ginger, on its own to cleanse your palate between fish, should be eaten with chopsticks.

Another popular form of sushi is sashimi, which is fish with no rice. Sashimi is appropriate for chopsticks, and a small amount of wasabi or soy sauce may be dabbed on the corners, but more than a small amount will overwhelm the flavor of the fish.

Corson contends that you may even see Japanese people eating sushi with chopsticks, but it remains technically incorrect.

Sushi is generally made to be eaten in one bite, but if that's a bit much for you, you may ask the chef to cut it for you. Master sushi chef Naomichi Yasuda of Sushi Yasuda in New York City advises that the flavors and textures of the piece are carefully crafted to be enjoyed in one bite. Try using your thumb and index finger to pick up the morsel. Yasuda agrees with Corson that soy sauce and wasabi should never be mixed in a sauce, but should "meet together" on your palate. In 2000, *New York Times* critic William Grimes called Sushi Yasuda "sublime," so we can assume Yasuda knows what he's talking about.

To cap off the meal, don't skip the tea, as a cup will help your body metabolize the salt from the soy sauce. And though it's more common knowledge thanks to the film *Mr. Baseball*, it is considered a bad omen to leave your chopsticks standing vertically in your rice, so only do that if your intention *was* to creep out the entire staff and possibly the other patrons. Another etiquette rule from Japanese culture is never pass food with chopsticks. This is reminiscent of traditional cremation processes after a death—the small body remnants not rendered to ash by burning were separated via chopsticks. You're probably extremely hungry for raw fish now that you've thought of that!

# Serving Wine

## Your reds are too warm and your whites are too cold

Everyone knows red wine is served at room temperature, and white wine is chilled. So your reds get stored, your whites go in the fridge, and both come straight out for guests, perfect as is. Except this standard isn't based on a temperature-controlled home and a refrigerator—it dates back to the time of castles and wine cellars. Now, you *might* actually live in a drafty old castle, but if you don't, you have probably served wine at the wrong temperature.

## HOW TO DO IT RIGHT

## Get out the thermometer

"Room temperature" isn't actually specific, which is the first problem for most people serving reds—both at home and in restaurants. And just to make it more of a challenge, different reds have slight variations of optimal serving temperatures. Wine Director Joseph Nase not only has a job you didn't know existed, but his article in "The Sommelier" section of *New York Magazine* detailed a temperature serving guide more complex than most knew existed. Pulling a Merlot out of the cabinet with a Chianti? For shame!

The darker the wine, the warmer its serving temperature. Full-bodied reds like Merlot, Shiraz, Pinot

Noir, Brunello, Barolo, port, and, Nase says, "truly great Burgundy whites, like Montrachet," should be served at 60–65°F. Because your home and many restaurants maintain a much more comfortable room temperature than a medieval castle, these wines are generally served too warm. The bottle should actually be cool to the touch, and Nase recommends about forty-five minutes in the fridge to get to the proper temp from your luxuriously warm home's room temperature.

Lighter, fruity reds, such as Chianti, Rioja, Valpolicella, and Chinon should be even cooler, served at 50–60°F, which means about an hour and a half in the fridge before serving.

Heavier whites should be slightly warmer than light whites. This means most white Burgundies (unless it's super fancy, then warmer is better), Chardonnays, Rieslings, and other high-quality dessert whites should be served at 50–60°F, like light reds. Your favorite Chard is losing flavor in that fridge, which is way colder than any wine cellar ever dreamed of being, so leave it out for an hour before serving.

Light and fruity whites such as Pinot Gris, Sauvignon Blanc, and light Australian whites should be served at 45–50°F. There's a decent range, but the average refrigerator temperature is 35–40°F, so even these light whites need some warm-up time between the fridge and serving.

Finally, really basic whites, including box wine, don't have "complex" flavor that can be ruined by cold, so if you're serving those straight out of the fridge, that's actually fine.

It's better to store wine in a place too cold than too warm, as Jon Bonné with MSNBC warns storing at room temperature may "speed the aging of the wine," and ruin the flavor.

Or just err on the side of caution, serving only cheap bottles of white from the fridge. Even simpler? Serve beer instead!

# Tapping a Keg

## The more handling, the more foam, and you're probably pump-happy

Having a little party for yourself and as many close personal friends as you can jam into a house? Or maybe you're making a kitchen or den a fountain of brewery abundance. Either way, you have a keg of beer that needs to be tapped. You bring it from the store, and carry/push it into the house singlehandedly, because that's part of the deal, right? You don't see lions getting help dragging a zebra across the plains. (Or do they? Um, whatever.) You know to jam the cap on and turn, and you're prepared for the inevitable beer shower that follows. That's fine, all part of the fun. You prime that pump with a bunch of enthusiastic presses like it's gym equipment. And when the fourth and fifth cups come out foamy, just drink 'em anyway.

Oh, crap. You want to move the keg into the other room. You're a pro at toting it by now, but your friend helps you grab it, the grip wet with beer, so it falls and . . . the tap's broken. At this point you probably realize . . . you did it wrong.

## Give your keg some space

Chill it, move it carefully, and you don't need to pump it 'til the stream of beer has become a tiny trickle. Most people over-handle their kegs, fail to chill them first, and just have way too much fun with that pump. The result is tons of foam, and even the most advanced keg-tapper will get a beer shower when tapping an over-handled keg. And although you've gotten used to shakin' that poor keg like a Polaroid picture, you just might not pay attention to where you set it up, which is a setup for failure. Moving the tapped keg makes it vulnerable to tap breakage, which just spoils everyone's fun.

- When you pick up your keg, swallow your pride and ask if you most definitely have the right tap. Taps vary for U.S. and imported beer, and a German beer might even have a different tap than a U.K. beer. Even a beer snob pro is still human, and just might have handed you the wrong tap, which will be a serious bummer when you try to tap the thing, can't, and the store is closed. Just be nice when double-checking, not *assuming* they screwed it up.
- Bring a friend, and take care transporting your keg. Some people get a pride chip on their shoulders and try to carry the keg themselves, which just leads to more jostling, which leads to wasting your brew (and time) in foam.
- Let it chill for at least two hours. Put the keg in a good, big plastic bucket with ice. Having the keg in a bucket will also help contain any potential mess, especially important when having a big party. Make sure your bucket o'keg is where you want it *before* you tap it, to avoid any breakage.
- Just pour out the first five-ish cups of foam. It's normal to have to "get to" the good stuff, just like

the bottom of the keg might not be so great (a.k.a. "swill").

- Beer snobs will tell you the average person has a little too much fun with the pump. Over-pumping your keg will give you a foamy cup, so take it easy and only pump a few times when the beer stream is thin.

Handle with care, keep it chilled, and don't go too crazy with the pump, and you're already doing it better than most. You can even give yourself a pat on the back for going green—kegs are easily refurbished, and can last thirty years. So tap that keg as your good deed of the weekend, and now you can do it right.

# Tipping at Restaurants

## Fifteen percent is the *minimum* for decent service, and only for low-cost restaurants

There's nothing like tipping restaurant servers to bring out some awkward interactions socially. It's something many people disagree on—do you tip for bad service? What about mediocre service, when it was nothing special? How about when you feel the waiter was trying just a little too hard—why did he touch your arm? But you know, 15 percent is the standard for good service, so you stick with that. In fact, just 15 percent across the board seems pretty safe. Unless you had to wait a long time for your food, then you feel all right about leaving half of that. Or if the food is really expensive, do you have to go all the way to 15 percent, 'cause that's a *lot* of money for just bringing the food out. In fact, the waiter didn't even bring the food out, a food runner did! Eh, 12 percent will do without looking embarrassingly cheap, right?

## Get a crowbar and pry open your wallet

Fifteen percent is generally considered the lowest possible percentage for good service. Many people have a problem with tipping, because they feel the price of the food should suffice and it's not their responsibility to pay the waitstaff—the restaurant should. They may have a point in theory, but the way it works in the United States is that often the waitstaff are essentially independent contractors living off tips, and one person stiffing them isn't going to change the system.

But what about minimum wage? Servers get that anyway, right? Usually, no, but it varies from state to state, and a surprising number of states pay only $2.13 an hour to tipped employees. Technically, the tips the employee receives are supposed to add up to the minimum, but it's a difficult thing for a server to enforce, and usually a stiffed server just worked for nothing. When one accounts for taxes, many servers don't receive a paycheck at all, meaning they are essentially (but not legally) *independent contractors*, whose entire income is reliant on tips.

Most people feel 15 percent is a good tip, but according to manners expert Emily Post, it's actually the minimum percentage of what you should leave, with the "acceptable" range being 15 to 20 percent of the pre-tax bill. But the old 15 percent (which, once again, is the *minimum*) actually only applies to low-cost restaurants. In nicer restaurants, the servers have more people (food runners, hosts, table bussers) with whom to share their tips, so the percentage goes up to 20 to 25 percent. That's right—25 percent at a nice restaurant isn't so much "generous" (though it will feel it, at those prices) but *the norm*.

In an economic recession, tipped workers see a huge dip in their incomes, as people making less money are more likely to scrutinize or be critical of how they value a certain service. And the real kicker to that is, statistically, people don't actually tip on how great their service was. They are usually not aware of it, but tips are increased according to gender, attractiveness, and personality. This doesn't mean women make more than men—it means women are more likely to tip men higher than women, and men are more likely to tip women higher than men. A more extroverted server is more likely to earn a higher tip than an understated but impeccable server. And that whole bit in *Office Space*, where Jennifer Aniston's waitress character was constantly, obnoxiously "encouraged" by her boss to wear more flair? Brace yourselves: Not only is that a real thing, it *actually works*. A study by Michael Lynn at Cornell University and Michael Hall from Ithaca College found that "wearing something unusual" was one of the tricks that worked to increase tips. The full list of tip-increasing tricks from the study was:

- Wear something unusual.
- Introduce yourself by name.
- Sell, sell, sell. (Upsell food and beverage for a larger bill and thus, tip.)
- Squat next to the table.
- Touch your customers.
- Entertain your customers.
- Repeat customers' orders.
- Call your customers by name.
- Draw on the check.
- Use credit card insignia on tip trays and check folders.
- Smile.
- Write "Thank You" on the check.
- Forecast good weather.
- Give customers candy.

Some exceptions to these rules apply. People didn't really care for male servers drawing something cute on the checks, and African Americans were apt to tip *less* if the server touched them. If your server is doing anything that makes you uncomfortable, you do have the freedom to adjust your tip, but it will be viewed unkindly. If you're with a group, you may be stuck with an 18 percent gratuity added by the management. Like upscale restaurants, groups are expected to tip a higher percentage.

Whether you care what Emily Post has to say about etiquette or not, bear in mind next time you leave a tip that it may very well be your server's only wage, which she probably has to share with other people. Even "cheaper" restaurant servers usually have to "tip out" the table bussers, host, or *somebody*, and very rarely get to keep all their tips.

# Using Utensils

**Maybe you know the difference between a shrimp fork and a salad fork, but you don't always have to *use* that knowledge, because the best utensils are already attached to your hands**

It's a social nightmare to be at a fancy dinner and use the salad fork for your entrée. Your mother would be horrified . . . or maybe not your mom, but at least a great aunt or something. Seriously, *someone* would be horrified, and the music would crash to a halt with a record scratch, and an upscale lady would faint. No, but really, you don't want to look like you just crawled out of a cave while enjoying some fancy fare, right? Some chef put care into that food, and it's an *art*, so the least you can do is use the right fork, and move it from your plate to your mouth in the best way possible.

"The best way possible," however, is probably with your fingers.

## HOW TO DO IT RIGHT

### Use your God-given utensils

Chef Roy Choi told *The New York Times* one of the awesomest things ever about his encouragement of patrons eating with their hands at his restaurant, A-Frame: "You eat with conviction and passion when using your hands. I hope that people let their guard down and throw out some of the rules we have regarding etiquette and connect like animals."

Oh, was that not a fantastic enough argument for eating with your fingers? Okay, fine, for a little more on the subject of cutlery abandon, let's look at the history of how we ended up using the typical fork, knife, and spoon. The fork was first used in ancient Greece to aid in carving meat, not transporting it to your mouth, but it eventually evolved to being used by royalty in the seventh-century Middle East, and slowly spread through Europe. Emphasis on slowly. When British traveler and writer Thomas Coryate first brought a fork to England from Italy, it was mocked as being "too feminine" and unnecessary. As forks were developed in France to have the more practical four prongs instead of the traditional and more cumbersome two, they once again slowly came into prominence, but were not used commonly in the United States until well into the 1800s.

The spoon has a more prominent history, dating back to prehistoric humans using shells or wood scraps as spoons. Spoons made of gold, horn, or silver were used by wealthy families in the Middle Ages. When they could be produced with cheaper materials such as pewter, spoons became common items. The knife has long been common, too, dating back to prehistoric times, but the idea of a knife strictly for table use didn't evolve until after the Middle Ages. So the spoon and knife have a rich history, but when you add the fork, never mind three different kinds of forks, you can see our modern eating utensil setup is, historically speaking, somewhat new. So new, some finger-lickin' purists think it's already starting to go out of fashion, and for a variety of reasons.

Modern critics of cutlery, such as New York chef Marcus Samuelsson, will point out that it is specifically a phenomenon in Western culture, and in parts of Asia, Africa, and the Middle East, using hands as utensils is the norm. Los Angeles chef Jet Tila of Bistronomics credits hands-only eating with lifting diners' moods by evoking the memory of childhood eating with our fingers. The Surreal Gourmet, Bob Blumer, thinks eating with your fingers increases the eating experience by incorporating the sense of touch to help you better appreciate the texture and temperature of your meal. Nutrition author Mark Sisson points out that our hands remain the most dexterous utensil available to us.

Cookbook author Julie Sahni is a native of India, where eating with the thumb, pointer, and index fingers of your right hand is the proper etiquette; she finds a fork to be "like a weapon." When she first came to Europe as a touring dancer, she learned how to use utensils properly so as not to be rude, but never enjoyed using them. Like most Indians, she still extols the value of eating with your hands and how it "evokes great emotion . . . It kindles something very warm and gentle and caressing."

If you're not ready to try it out in public, try eating with your hands at home. If you enjoy it, many Indian and Ethiopian restaurants are cutlery-free, as well as crab restaurants and sushi bars. The phenomenon of American-style food being served without cutlery has hit New York and Los Angeles with force, so keep an eye out for it to reach your town as well.

# WORK AND FINANCE

# Wearing Business Casual

## Too big and way, way too casual

"Business casual" may have a different definition in every human resources office in the United States, but it does have some expectations that generally stay firm . . . firm to firm. To your old office, "business casual" might have meant you don't need to wear a tie with your suit, but in your new office, someone is wearing *jeans*. Game on—you come to work the next day in your favorite T-shirt, but now there are some chuckles behind your back, because your favorite T-shirt has a teddy bear on it (this has happened), and no one realized you were being ironic, so now you're pretty much the Norman Bates of the office. What's that, Mother? Oh yes, dress for success.

## HOW TO DO IT RIGHT
## Stay classy

Stop dressing so casually. The number one complaint of both fashion experts and bosses is that most people take the casual in business casual way too far, and things digress to graphic T-shirts and socks with sandals. Graphic tees and sandals communicate "I like watching TV and playing Frisbee in the park with my dog." Duh, everyone likes that. Even with a lax HR department, the thing you want to communicate at all times is "I get the job done."

Jeans can be acceptable, so long as they are in excellent shape and fit well—not baggy, no rips, and the current trend is a darker wash is considered dressier. Make sure you wear nice (not white!) socks, because often pants hike up when you sit, and no one needs to be distracted by your ankle skin. T-shirts are acceptable if they are on the dressier side—graphic tees are almost universally judged as juvenile, so leave them out of the office, even on casual Friday. "Graphic" tends to include large brand names, which are distracting and unprofessional.

The second major complaint, namely from the fashion side, (because execs might not consciously notice) is that even people who grasp the idea of an appropriate level of casual often wear clothing that's just too big. If your button-down is untucked, and if the shirt covers most of your crotch, it's too big. If the shirt has a boxy fit, and you pair it with pleated-front pants, you're lost in a sea of fabric waves. You don't need to be slim to wear a slim-cut shirt; look for a nice button-down oxford that doesn't give you fabric love handles when you tuck it in. That's right—tuck it in. If it looks bad tucked in, you're doing it wrong.

Keep bringing new options to the dressing room until you find one that looks good and fits well. Puffs and pulls mean it doesn't fit well. Sleek and smooth with a nice, close drape is more what you're shooting for. Speaking of drape, it seriously doesn't hurt to look at Don Draper. The wardrobe department of *Mad Men* is notorious for not only its gruelingly meticulous attention to the details of the period, but impeccable fits for every actor down to the extras. Don Draper's shirt never puffs at the tuck nor bunches around buttons.

Although women tend to fare slightly better than men under the harsh gaze of a fashion expert sizing up business casual, they often have the opposite problem—too short, too tight, or too much cleavage. Save it for the club! Or at home with your cat and some microbrews, it really doesn't matter, so long as you're not flaunting the goods at the office. Just 'cause it all worked out for Erin Brockovich doesn't mean it will for you.

One hint that you can take from your jeans and graphic T-shirt (that you're totally not wearing to work now, right?) is: cotton. At least, natural fabrics and natural fabric blends are generally more "breathable" than synthetics, and will help you avoid pit stains. And no matter how hot it gets, do not resort to sandals or flips-flops. No one wants to see your toes, and socks with summer footwear looks ridiculous. You really can find a nice, casual, breathable shoe that will look a billion times better than a sandal. Don't do it. It doesn't matter if everyone else in the office is doing it. What's that, Mother? If all my friends wore sandals and flip-flops to the office and then jumped off a bridge, would I too?

# Hiring People

## Hiring people too much like yourself, or hiring friends and family

"Listen to your heart," is a decent piece of wisdom, because we all know our minds can trick us, and sometimes you need to go with your gut. When it comes to hiring, and you work for a company, you're going to gravitate toward hiring people you get along with. Because they "get" you, and that's so important with all the projects on your slate in the upcoming year. You want a hire that will be your extra arm—and eyes, and ears. If you didn't have to work with this person, you would definitely hang out. Maybe you end up doing just that. This is perfect! How about if you work for yourself, and you need to hire some help? Your best friend is out of work, how perfect! Or maybe your cousin, sister, or parent is looking for a new gig. Awesome! You can get them on the cheap, maybe even under the table, and you know you like them. You can't imagine the nightmare of hiring people you didn't *like*. After all, you have to be around them for forty hours a week, maybe more. This is all gonna work out.

Unless it doesn't, and it often won't. In which case, you've got quite a problem.

## HOW TO DO IT RIGHT

# Tell your heart to quiet down so you can hear your brain

Don't hire friends, family, or the person you *like* most. As harsh and unpleasant as that sounds, it comes straight from the mouth of gazillionaire entrepreneur Richard Branson. Our brains are wired to gravitate toward what's familiar, and what is more familiar to you than . . . you? What we think of as "liking" sometimes might be more accurately described as "finding comfort in its familiarity."

So let's say you're hiring for a company, which you work for, but don't own. When interviewing candidates, you and your hardwired brain are going to gravitate toward the person most like yourself *even if you don't consciously realize it.* But you probably will, citing your ability to get along with and understand this potential new hire as the reasons you want him working with you.

The problem with that is, someone who is like you is likely to make the same choices you make. Fantastic, right? No. It's fantastic if it's your partner, sibling, or roommate, but when it comes to business, you're much better off hearing a different perspective and being forced into seeing a perception other than your own. This will diversify the scope of your project, and open doors you perceived as solid walls. Have you ever been searching for your lost keys, and a friend finds them for you immediately? Those "fresh eyes" are great for the business world, and someone who "sees" like you see is less likely to, um, see a superior choice to which you were blind. See?

The issue shifts a little when it comes to you hiring someone for your own company or startup. After all, hiring family worked out for Donald Trump, and entrepreneur Mike Repole (Glacéau, Pirate Brands snacks, and Energy Kitchen) has hired more than a dozen of his old buddies. But Virgin's Richard Branson advises against it, telling *Entrepreneur*, "As tempting as it may be to staff your new business with friends and relatives, this is likely to be a serious mistake."

Branson points to the difficulty of a situation in which the friend or family member doesn't work out. He advises you should hire someone who already knows the industry well, and "shares your vision." An article in *USA Today* argued that hiring friends and family can be "boon or bust" because good old familiarity tells us to trust them more. If you think, damn the torpedoes, I'm hiring family anyway, make sure you set firm expectations and stay logical, professional, and realistic about their abilities. Also be prepared to deal with the fallout that's possible—hostile family dinners, your friends and family taking sides, and losing a relationship entirely. If you're willing to roll those dice, by all means, be realistic about your odds.

# Facing Deadlines

## You've heard of Murphy's Law, but now Hofstadter's Law is in full effect!

You have a deadline coming up, and it's pretty tough. You're excited about the opportunity, and panicked about the workload. So you get yourself together. It's a matter of simple math, right? You need to estimate the number of hours in the job, and the number of hours you have to complete it. Then you can figure in minor details like sleeping and eating.

So you begin . . . well, you feel behind today, but you just have to make it up with more work tomorrow, right? Then you're back on track! But then your best friend calls you, stranded on the side of the road, and your water heater breaks. That's okay! It's okay! You just have to make up the time in the next two days. Then you get a cold in the middle of July, and can't think or speak Englishtalk good. But . . . it's okay . . . it's . . . okay . . . you have like, one more day to make up all this work. A whole twenty-four hours. For two weeks of work. You can do it . . . you just . . . need more coffee, right?

Murphy's Law may say what can go wrong, will go wrong, but Mr. Hofstadter hit the nail on the head with his law: It will always take longer than you think it will, even when you account for the fact that you *know* it will take longer than you think it will.

## HOW TO DO IT RIGHT

## Less planning, more doing

Hofstadter's Law, which states that a task will always take more time than you think—*even* when you account for the fact it will do just that—is named for writer Douglas Hofstadter, who created the term. The problem with planning is, you can't plan for the unforeseen. You can't even schedule in "minus two days for the unforeseen" because statistically, you will use up all the time you've allowed yourself no matter what, as if the goal was an ever-expanding gas filling whatever size room is available to it. Or one of those weird iguanas you got as a kid that just *kept growing* to fit whatever size cage/habitat you gave it. Yes, your goal is an ill-advised acquisition of a pet iguana, and it will just keep growing, watching you and being kinda creepy until it reaches its maximum enclosure, a.k.a. the due date.

This expansion-to-fit time theory is known as Parkinson's Law, after a humorous bit written by Cyril Northcote Parkinson in 1955 in *The Economist*, in which he joked about a math equation that demonstrated the rate at which bureaucracies expand over time. It's still used in terms of government, but over time started to also mean *stuff* filling whatever time allotment it's given.

When it comes to your deadline, you can try to follow the common wisdom: Plan carefully to finish *early*, and be aware of your flexibility. You're not going to do any good driving yourself into the ground creating an inferior product that just happens to be on time. Knowing if your deadline has any flexibility will tell you if you're the Sydney Opera House, finishing ten years late, or Douglas Brinkley, the biographer of

Jack Kerouac who had to return his $200,000 advance when he missed his deadline (*On The Road*'s fiftieth anniversary).

Once you know the basics—time, strictness of deadline, division of big project into little projects to create the whole—stop the constant planning and revision, and just keep your nose to the grindstone. I'm talking to highly sensitive people in particular, who probably just cringed even as they read the term "highly sensitive people," because they are more likely to feel anxiety from the pressure—and said anxiety can manifest in all sorts of fun distractions like spontaneous housecleaning, insomnia, and tear-filled collapses. All of which could have been avoided if you delicately crawled out of the nightmare pit that is your own mind and just focused on the task at hand. So yes, that means stop planning, because the more you spin your wild calculations of $x$ being accomplished in $y$ time, the less you are focused on *actually doing*. Even if the worst-case scenario comes down, and you fail something really important, at least you will have failed *less*.

# Increasing Productivity

## Staying inside to get more work done will result in *less* work done than if you'd taken your lunch break out in the park

You have a ton of work to get done in too few hours—again. Looks like you'll be burning the midnight oil. Gotta keep your head down and your nose to the grindstone. You're not leaving your office until all the work is done. You're devoted to the cause, and you're determined to produce a mass amount of work. The problem is, by the time you're 60 percent done, you're 100 percent burnt out.

## Get some air

Get out of the office, and take a quick break out in nature, observing it. Multiple studies on attention restoration theory (ART), most notably by Stephen Kaplan, have been focusing on attention as it was first published by William James in 1892, describing attention as both involuntary (in which attention is captured by "inherently intriguing or important stimuli") and voluntary a.k.a. "directed attention" (in which attention is "directed by cognitive-control processes").

Kaplan found urban environments demand your directed attention, whereas being in nature will "invoke involuntary attention modestly." By switching to the nature-induced attention type, you restore your directed attention reserves. So next time you think it's a good idea to work through your lunch break, guess again—you'll get more done by the end of the day if you take the break, go outside, and find a tree. Even worse would be skipping that hike to sneak in some weekend work.

What if you can't take a walk in the park? Researchers have found the bizarrely technical answer to finding nature is . . . use more tech to replicate it. Download nature sounds, watch nature videos online—that media still uses your "directed attention." Without a little nature, you're simply going to get less done.

The walk doesn't even have to be enjoyable. Yes, you can have a bad time, like having a pigeon poop on your shoulder or being freezing cold the whole time. It doesn't matter! So drop the excuses, because happiness doesn't seem to be the key in attention restoration. Even if you just witnessed your newly washed car being "decorated" profusely by the local birds, observing said birds just reset your attention, no matter how angry or grossed out you felt—you still used indirect attention. Study subjects who tromped around in the cold and reported being unhappy with the experience still had increased performances. Even more helpful, unlike walking for fitness, it's a one-shot deal. You don't need to do it every day to build a cumulative benefit—you benefit immediately after doing it.

Can you find another way to switch up your attention types? Probably, but for some unknown reason, time with nature provided better cognitive function improvement than other quiet activities. A study from the University of Michigan in 2008 theorized that a person's preconceived positive notions about nature may play into its mega-restorative power, but that's only a theory. For all we know, nature may be chock full of microscopic faeries that just make you feel really good, in which case, you totally owe an apology to that dude at Burning Man who told you all of this years ago.

# Putting in Longer Hours

## Working more than eleven hours a day more than doubles your risk of depression and heart disease, and you actually accomplish less

A few old sayings have been floating around for so long, they must be true. Like "hard work never killed anyone" and "butt in chair = work." So it's hard to disagree when management insists on everyone putting in extra hours to ramp up productivity levels. The more hours your butt is in the seat, the more work produced, right? You know at hour ten, you start making increasingly stupid mistakes, and at hour twelve you can't resist checking a few personal things online, and by hour thirteen . . . well, now it's all a bit of a mess. But you still got more accomplished than if you'd worked an eight hour day, surely.

First of all: Stop calling me Shirley. Second of all, you might just have accomplished *less* than in an eight-hour day.

### HOW TO DO IT RIGHT

## Eight is great

Work an eight-hour day and no more. Statistically, a seven-hour day would be just as productive, as the majority of work is produced between the second and sixth hours at work. Your boss not jumping for that idea? Maybe it's time to anonymously slip some studies into the suggestion box. And under her office door. And in the coffee room. And by the copier.

The studies that have been done involved English white-collar workers, so there may be some variation according to culture and job type, but scientists expect broader studies to reflect similar findings. It wasn't a quickie study either. The "Whitehall II" studies led by Professor Mika Kivimäki and Marianna Virtanen have been ongoing since 1985 and take into account tons of other factors, such as the subjects' fitness levels and smoking habits. Turns out no matter what, working long shifts makes you twice as likely to suffer from depression, and 67 percent more likely to develop coronary heart disease.

If you think long shifts leading to depression and heart disease are for coal miners only, remember these are *white-collar* studies, in which the people working the longest hours were the most "successful," making the most money, and earning the most prestigious titles. All they have to trade for that is their joy and heart!

It sounds like a deal with the devil right out of a Victorian gothic novel, complete with a feather quill pen in your hand and a contract before your face, and the vague smell of sulfur. But just like Ol' Scratch's tricks of literary fame, that too is only an illusion, because working long hours actually makes you do less work, and reduces quality. Back in 1914 Henry Ford got the almost angelic idea to double his employees' pay and cut their work hours to eight per day. The rest of the industrial world—including the National Association of Manufacturers—got unsurprisingly nervous, and angry at him. But basically their heads exploded as Ford enjoyed record productivity. His competitors later had to adopt his model to keep up.

Ford didn't come up with the less-is-more hourly idea, however. In fact, British Parliament passed a ten-hour workday law in 1848 and saw increased productivity. By the 1890s the norm had dropped to eight hours and productivity further increased. After Ford's success, the eight-hour-a-day rule became standard, not out of kindness to the worker, but for the overall benefit of the company, which was enjoying more productivity for less money.

The science of all those decades was pushed aside, ironically enough, by the sci-tech workers of the Silicon Valley, starting in the 1970s. As they took on odd hours and their industry boomed, their "work ethic" of longer hours crept into the rest of the United States. Eventually working long hours became a bragging-rights badge of work-ethic passion, and both companies and employees came to expect it. No one seemed to care that the science of the eight-hour workday hadn't changed, and the protests of productivity experts went unheard.

Slowly, we are rebounding from the late seventies, and workers are pushing back against longer hours, albeit carefully due to an unfortunate economy for change. The bright side is, science supports both sides—with shorter shifts, the worker is healthier and more productive. It does seem to be oddly up to employees to bring this to the attention of management, but let's be honest—it's not the first or last time you do your bosses' work for them.

# Saving Money

## Putting money into an account that accrues no interest; using a bank instead of a credit union

You carefully take a little slice of each paycheck for your savings account. A bunch of your friends have no savings, and some other friends lost a bunch of cash in the stock market, so you are riding high with some money in your savings! Although it's true that having any savings puts you ahead of 60 percent of the U.S. population, if you're just dropping it in an account (like your checking) that doesn't pay you interest you're doing it wrong.

## HOW TO DO IT RIGHT

## Get interest-ed

Utilize premium savings accounts and certificates of deposit (CDs), preferably with a credit union, which unlike your bank is not-for-profit. Credit union employees say that many people have a tendency to deposit everything into their checking accounts so it's readily available, as savings accounts often have limited access. But by having your extra funds available, you're more likely to spend them.

A good savings strategy can be using a certificate of deposit, in which you deposit a certain amount of money for a specific amount of time, during which it accrues interest. CDs are especially popular for parents saving for their kid's college—yup, even if that kid isn't on solid foods yet. The money is insured by the Federal Deposit Insurance Corporation, so unlike stocks, it's virtually risk-free. But also unlike stocks, it has no chance of showing you an awesome return. You may have already figured out that putting *all* your assets into stocks might be thrilling in that totally dangerous sort of way, but sometimes you need the rock of low return and low risk.

"Risk tolerance" is the key to how you should save versus investing and spending. John MacDonald, the Vice President of Corporate Strategy for Lupoli Companies (a company often credited with the revitalization of Massachusetts former "mill towns" Lowell and Lawrence), advises you examine your stage in life to find your risk tolerance. "If you happen to be a younger person with little or no responsibility," MacDonald says, "then you probably have a greater risk tolerance than someone saving who has two kids or who is retired or getting ready to retire."

It's more reasonable to assess your risk tolerance than taking the old-timey advice to put everything you can in savings. If you have a little you can risk in the stock market, then it might be worth the risk *and* return. MacDonald admits he takes more risk with his money than he would with his children's college fund. A CD might not be "as fruitful" as the stock market, but it is safe. Some people are "spenders" and others are "riskers," but they're not necessarily doing it right, depending on what stage of life they are in.

Another major advantage to saving is using a credit union instead of a bank. Fred Baker, the president of the National Association of Credit Unions, told *The Huffington Post*, "Consumer frustration with Wall

Street motivated people to explore the value of Main Street credit unions."

Credit union memberships doubled between 2010 and 2011 as consumers grew increasingly wary of banks and their fees. Because credit unions are not-for-profit collectives run by the members, they are able to offer better deals than banks, which are owned by outside shareholders.

For people who are used to banks, the first major downside is the lack of convenient ATMs. But if you're using a credit union for savings, theoretically you shouldn't need much ATM action. If you decide to keep your checking at a credit union as well, you may find paying the occasional ATM fee is still cheaper than bank fees. Some credit unions have fewer services than banks, but as their popularity expands, so does their range of services. (Oh, and more ATMs too!)

Assess your risk tolerance—if you've been socking it all away, maybe it's time to play the market . . . responsibly, because it does bear a resemblance to gambling. If you've been throwing it all in checking, switch to savings and give a credit union a chance. And if you're not saving anything, you are like the majority of the population, but even putting away $10 a week would give you a small emergency cushion. Much like when sitting through a long baseball game, even a small cushion is way better than no cushion. Switch into a premium savings account or CDs to get a handful more padding—every little bit helps.

# Paying Off Your Credit Cards

## Most people prefer to eliminate the debt on one card completely, but often the largest debt should be paid down

You had to use your credit more than you would have liked, but at least you got through school. You also got through clothing, late night pizza delivery, and several friends' weddings. Now your balances are rising and you want to improve your credit score and get the debt monkey off your back. You carefully pay off the smallest card first—one card down, three to go! It feels great to eliminate an entire debt!

Feels great, yes. The most effective? No.

## Look for the biggest—debt *and* interest

Almost everyone prefers to pay off an entire small card than to keep subtracting drops from the bucket of a large debt, but research from Moty Amar, Scott Rick, and colleagues has found the most efficient way to handle debt and the psychological response to paying debt are at odds.

Multiple studies have found people seriously underestimate how much interest adds up on their credit debt, and don't look at the whole of their debt, but rather card by card. Part of the reason for this is that our brains are wired to divide and conquer, breaking a large task into small ones to complete it. By the same token, we are apt to want to pay off an entire debt, rather than saving on interest by reducing the largest debt.

Amar, Rick, et al. in their study "Winning the Battle but Losing the War: The Psychology of Debt Management," came up with the term "debt account aversion." People feel better paying off an entire account, although often it defies the clear logic of paying down the greatest debt with the greatest interest. Other studies dating back to the 1930s show that as we get closer to achieving a goal, our motivation in regards to the goal greatly increases. Paying off a larger debt often takes years, so we have less motivation than we would for that glorious moment of cutting up a paid-off, smaller card.

Even some financial experts have advised paying off small debts first, for a fast victory, known as the "debt-snowball method" (the idea being one paid-off account helps "snowball" into all debts being paid off). Although the rush of paying off a card might inspire some people to keep at the payments, science doesn't find the motivation lasts—and then the consumer is stuck with more interest than if he had put the same money on a greater debt.

In fact, people are working really hard to *not* pay off debt correctly. The "Battle" study found most consumers work really hard to get rid of the smallest amount of debt, but research shows that the only way to prevent people from clearing an entire debt over reducing the greatest-interest debt was to make sure they didn't have enough to wipe out the *entire* small debt. Without the incentive of completely eliminating the account, people lost the temptation to pay down the small debt instead of the larger ones, and actually made better financial decisions.

Much like eliminating the temptation of paying off a small debt, the study found debt consolidation was also likely to keep people on track with "financially optimal" pay-off choices. However, the researchers caution you to be wary with debt consolidation, as balance transfer fees may be attached that can actually increase what you owe in interest.

# Multitasking

## Complete one task before moving on to the next

When you're writing a report, having a text conversation, and answering your phone at the same time, it can be somewhat annoying. But when you realize you're actually handling these things, you feel like you just piloted the *Millennium Falcon* through an asteroid field. You're getting so much done . . . it just happens to be of poor quality.

## You're better off moving from one task to the next than trying to do multiple tasks at the same time, especially when multimedia are involved

Even teenagers who seem so breezy about maintaining several instant message conversations while watching TV and cranking out some homework suffered poor performances under scientific study. In fact, regular multimedia multitaskers had *worse* performances when multitasking under scientific observation than "low multitaskers," due to their compete inability to ignore interferences. The multitaskers were particularly vulnerable to distraction—and not even good distractions. Pretty much anything distracted them. In fact, chances are if you made it through this entire paragraph in one try, you are *not* a frequent multitasker.

Stanford's Professor Clifford Nass, one of the authors of a 2009 multitasking study, went in search of the benefits of multitasking—and didn't find any. Nass and colleagues had a few theories in the beginning, for example, that multitaskers would have better memories due to higher storage commensurate with higher task load. But when put to the test, the high multitaskers failed and were highly outperformed in memory by the low multitaskers. Eyal Ophir, another study author, reported on the memory tests: "The high multitaskers were doing worse and worse the further they went along because they kept seeing more letters and had difficulty keeping them sorted in their brains."

Nass then figured perhaps high multitaskers would be more adept at switching tasks than low multitaskers. That turned out to be giving the high multitaskers way too much credit, because they failed hardcore. When switching between tasks, it turned out their minds were still on a previous task. They had a hard time letting go and—ohhh! A butterfly!

The scientists didn't actually release butterflies, but it's pretty obvious that's what the high multitaskers' reactions would have been. Not only were they not able to tear themselves away from irrelevant information, they were less able to "filter" the irrelevant stuff out, and then they weren't able to dismiss irrelevant information to focus on the important things.

So what factors into whether or not someone can multitask? It depends on whom you ask. Some research suggests that age is a relevant factor, whereas other studies have found "mindset" to be an important factor in the failure of multitasking. Mindset is the mental state a certain task requires for you to make appropriate judgments or take the right actions. Arguing (ahem, *discussing*) with your significant other requires an entirely different mindset than writing a TPS report for work—but if you're multitasking and switching between mindsets, you're exhausting your mind much faster than you would if you kept a consistent mindset. If a person becomes mentally exhausted from this mindset switching, she will stay in one mindset and thus not make the best decisions or produce the best work where a different mindset is required.

Just in case multitasking didn't seem doomed enough to failure, another study tromps along telling us multitasking is also making us fat. Really! A 2011 study by R. E. Oldham-Cooper and colleagues found performing tasks (that means even playing solitaire) while having a meal caused people to feel *less full* than nonmultitaskers, even though everyone in the study had eaten the same amount. Multitaskers were also more likely to snack—almost twice as much as those who had eaten their lunches without distraction.

Nass and company's multitasking survey summed it up well: "In short, when an employee must wear multiple hats, she should try to change hats as infrequently as possible." If your job won't allow you to stop multitasking, delegate your task switching carefully, and don't burn out on simple things like sending thirty-eight texts to sort out your dinner plans. Whenever possible, only navigate one asteroid field at a time.

# Buying Happiness

## You *can* buy a certain degree of happiness, so long as you choose experiences over material goods, enjoy anticipation, and a few other key tips

Money can't buy you love, or happiness, or a beach house. No wait, it definitely buys you a beach house. Which would probably make you pretty happy. But in the past, you found money's ability to buy you happiness was limited and easily fades. Even the best video gaming system will occasionally collect dust, even though you were sure it wouldn't. There's always a time when a sports car is actually just a tool to get you from point A to point B.

But you *can* buy happiness, if you buy it right.

## HOW TO DO IT RIGHT

### Listen to (and purchase with) your heart

Once again, we're not as good at predicting our future feelings as we think we are. We fail to make the financial choices that will make us the happiest over the choices *we think will* make us happiest. Whoops.

In the hilariously titled study, "If money doesn't make you happy, then you're probably not spending it right," researchers Elizabeth Dunn, Daniel Gilbert, and Timothy Wilson compiled a myriad of past studies and polls to find eight key tips to "buying happiness." Here's what they determined:

- Purchase experiences rather than goods. People tend to fondly remember a vacation more than feeling thrilled every time they use an antique armoire. Memories are the "purchasable" that continue to generate pleasure with time, far more than goods, which people often *assume* will continuously make them happy, which statistically isn't true.
- Be charitable. People feel better when spending on others, rather than themselves, just as old Scrooge found out, but you don't need three ghosts to figure that out. Under MRI studies, people giving away money to a food bank had brain activity in the same areas as people receiving awards. This "better to give than to receive" feeling also extended to giving to friends and romantic partners.
- Many small > one big. Although most people estimate one big purchase would make them happy, most people are wrong. Multiple small purchases were found to generate more pleasure than one large purchase. One of the reasons for this is the time between various pleasurable purchases keeps us from getting used to or "adapting to" it and minimizing how awesome it feels.
- Warranties and insurance displease us. It's common sense that warranties and insurance keep us enjoying an item, right? Seems logical, but the opposite is true when it comes to *feelings*. Turns out the "prospect of loss" we have associated with an insured item dampens our enjoyment. In studies where people were given the option of returning an item and others were given no return option, the

no-return-option people had a higher estimation of the item.

- Enjoy later but purchase now. The exact opposite of the popular "buy now, pay later," it turns out that one thing we really enjoy is the anticipation of something good. "Delaying consumption" also prevents us from making impulse buys that we may not be so happy about after consuming (like eight deep-fried candy bars at the fair). People chose unhealthy snacks to eat now, but when choosing snacks for the future, they chose healthy ones instead.

- Consider the mundane details. When thinking of an exciting purchase, people tend to *only* think about the excitement of the purchase, and not the mundane details surrounding it; therefore, they are ultimately disappointed when it becomes a reality and the boring details weren't factored into the equation. When daydreaming about dropping a wad of cash to visit your favorite theme park, you probably weren't thinking of finagling the parking lot, or that sweaty guy behind you in a long line who's never heard of personal space. Being realistic about your goal will actually leave you happier when it happens.

- Comparison shopping is a setup for a letdown. People use different comparisons when consuming a thing than when shopping for it. Sometimes comparing details keeps us from seeing the whole picture, and we "overestimate the hedonistic impact" of what society has deemed a more desirable item.

- Popularity matters. Statistically, we like something more when we see other people enjoying it as well. The happiness (or lack thereof) of people enjoying a thing we would like to also enjoy is indicative of how much *we* might enjoy said thing. Simple.

Who said money can't buy happiness? They probably weren't modern psychologists!

# Negotiating

## Don't argue, don't persuade

You're always ready for a good negotiation. It might be discussing a better price on a car from a fast-talking dealer you intend to outwit, or maybe you're trying to get a deal at a local yard sale on a vintage Power Ranger action figure. (So what if it's the pink one?) Because half the U.S. population considers themselves under-paid, you've probably thought of trying to negotiate a better salary at work. So you brainstormed a list of why you're worth more. You have a neat, bullet-pointed list that you're carefully committing to memory, ready to argue on behalf of your value. And they are really good points, too.

The problem is, when you offer an argument, the person with whom you're negotiating can't help but attempt to refute your points.

## Resist the urge to argue

There's an old saying about how the first person to throw out a number loses. But recent studies say you can throw out an initial offer—known as the anchor—and then field the counteroffer, which is called the adjustment, *without* offering arguments in favor of your offer. The problem with your arguments is, no matter how true and well crafted, they inspire a natural reaction of counterarguments, which will push you further away from your goal. Without your arguments, and without the responding counterarguments, you're statistically more likely to end up with a final result closer to your initial anchor.

In a negotiation, both parties involved see the other as an opponent, and as such the information supplied by "the enemy" is going to be viewed as such. Both people are looking for the ideal transaction *for themselves*, so it's not like any argument you make is going to cause a light bulb to go off over the other person's head and he will say, "Whoa, I hadn't taken that information into account and it's so true. Here, take everything you want!"

If only. Instead, your perfectly reasonable arguments are seen as suspect, and even the truest and most relevant information may be discarded. Still, any information you do present needs to be authentic, because any slip in your credibility will work against you. Most of all, you need to stay firm, and know your boundaries. It's okay to say "no" and walk away from the deal—negotiation writer Lee E. Miller points out that staying firm to the point of walking away "nicely" will "project confidence."

Miller points out that some people never outgrow needing to feel like they have "won." In these cases it is best to try to see from their perspective and see if there is a way to spin your negotiations so they think they *have* won. "Start from a place much further from where you want to end," Miller says. "This way, you can give up more without sacrificing what's important to you."

If you find yourself negotiating over e-mail, handle with care. If more than two people are involved in the negotiation—like a real estate deal—an e-mail chain can be handy to keep people in the loop. Some negotiation experts recommend e-mail, as it is more comfortable for many people and feels less confrontational. Others caution the opposite—that the lack of face-to-face, human-to-human interaction is likely to make people feel more comfortable about being jerks and making insulting offers. Make sure you never use all capital letters and multiple exclamation points, as these will take you into the argument zone. Be careful not to make an offensively low offer while emboldened by typing, or the whole deal may be called off entirely.

Most people have also assumed extroverts have the negotiation advantage, but Miller points out everyone should play to their personal strengths. An extrovert may end up talking over his opponent, and will be viewed unfavorably as a bully. An introverted person might be a better listener, and able to better "hear" the opposing point of view and carefully tailor her offer to meet it.

# Visualizing Positively

HOW YOU'RE DOING IT WRONG

## Although setting a positive intention is helpful, indulging in a positive fantasy actually decreased test subjects' energy

You might not be willing to admit it openly, but you have a vision board. You cut out images of specific things you'd like to bring into your life, and stare at them longingly in a dreamy haze. You fantasize about what it would be like to have great wealth. A mansion. A Smithers-release-the-hounds-size mansion. You can see this gorgeous abode clearly in your mind, you can feel the cool marble or the orate columns (hey, why not?) and the plush of the exotic rugs at your feet. You know if you keep staring at these images, and fantasizing about this mansion, pretty soon, you'll be living in it. Law of attraction, dude. Like attracts like.

Maybe it does, but you're still doing it wrong.

HOW TO DO IT RIGHT

## Put those intentions into action

Make sure your actions are in line with your goals. The whole "law of attraction" and "positive manifestation" movement has made itself a very comfy bed by being *impossible to disprove.* You didn't get that mansion you were visualizing? Well, apparently that's your fault for not wanting it hard enough, or purely enough, or for having a block. There's no way to argue with the "logic."

It's quite possible that thinking positively will bring more positive things into your life, and thinking negatively will bring more negative things into your life. There's a basic logic to it, as being constantly negative may keep you in a state of low mood, stress, and anxiety, which leads to a rash of other problems. There are undeniable and easily proven ways to demonstrate the power of thought. What cannot be demonstrated, however, is the power of thought to help you with something super-specific. In fact, many philosophers and spiritual people in the school of "law of attraction" are offended by the idea of using a principle that is really about spiritual development to, say, get yourself a mansion. Or any other physical thing, or entirely self-serving goal.

Of course, because it doesn't hold up to science, maybe visualizing that mansion *will* get you one— after all, no one can prove or disprove it. So what's the harm in a little fantasy?

NYU psychologists Heather Barry Kappes and Gabriele Oettingen have made the relatively counter-intuitive discovery that fantasizing about goals sapped test subjects' energy. The energy-vampire fantasies were those in which an idealized future plays out smoothly, without any indication of interruptions or deviations from perfection. Oddly enough, this extended beyond career and into romance. Study subjects who indulged in positive romantic fantasies about a crush were less likely to engage in a relationship with the person than subjects who didn't fantasize.

It seems that positive fantasies trick us into thinking these things have happened in a way that dampens our drive. Kappes and Oettingen found: "Positive fantasies about the future make energy seem unnecessary, and thus energy should not be mobilized."

Sounds like a downer, right? Like, now we can't even have awesome *fantasies*? Well, yes, you can, you just need to use them carefully. One benefit of positive fantasies was they lowered blood pressure, which isn't great for conquering the world, but is pretty great for conquering stress. So schedule your fantasy time when relaxation is important, and stay one step ahead of the problem Kappes and Oettingen encountered: Those who fantasize are less likely to act. Use any positive visualization to *power you forward into action*.

Dr. Douglas LaBier took to *Psychology Today* to warn the students of the Law of Attraction, or LOA, that the current way it's packaged is "a twisted and misunderstood version of an ancient spiritual perspective." But don't be too bummed, 'cause LaBier points out there's a difference between fantasies and envisioning. A fantasy is idealized and dreamy; envisioning is a mental formula of what things could look like. A healthy vision, LaBier points out, is one that uses "steps that require your mental, creative, emotional and strategic powers."

Purely egotistical goals are more likely to yield fantasy over envisioning—for example, wanting to improve your career in order to have lots of money to buy yourself toys versus a career that positively impacts your community. But if your heart is set on the toys, science says those fantasies are only pushing them to the ever-higher shelves above your head.

# RELATIONSHIPS AND SEX

# Kissing

## Underestimating its importance, not understanding the different gender perceptions of kissing—oh, and watch the tongue action

You've read all the articles since you were practically a kid. You know not to be too sloppy, not to be too reserved, and you know a fresh mouth is important. You'd never gag anyone, or lick her face like a puppy. You know not to be overly puckered, dry-mouthed, or leave painful bites (unless your partner is into that). You might be a technical kissing Casanova, but did you know you're creating a bond—or failing to create one? Do you know men's kissing motivations versus women's? An entire relationship (or just how awesome your weekend will be) may hang in the balance of your lips.

### HOW TO DO IT RIGHT

## Give kissing its due

"Never underestimate the power of a kiss," says sex therapist Dr. Sandra Scantling, adding "Kissing can be more intimate than intercourse." Research scientist Sheril Kirshenbaum refers to the results of a kiss as a "great chemical ballet," as dopamine gives kissers a sense of euphoria, as lips are our most "exposed erogenous zone." Oxytocin creates a sense of bonding for both males and females (not just for females as some had surmised in the past). The difficult part, of course, is that not all kisses produce euphoria or bonding. Kirshenbaum points out a kiss can make or break a relationship, as it sends signals to move closer or back away.

A study published in *Evolutionary Psychology* found significant differences in how men and women evaluated, used, and enjoyed kissing. The study found women used kissing to evaluate a potential sexual partner, whereas men were generally way more interested in getting past first base (truly shocking information). What the men generally didn't realize was, not only were they blowing their chances at further action by not placing more importance on the kissing, but that women responded to more sensitivities around kissing than men, such as the breath and taste of the male's mouth, as well as the appearance of his teeth. Men statistically cared less about those issues and were more concerned with the female's facial and body attractiveness.

Men and women also had different preferences for tongue contact in open-mouthed kisses. The majority of men believed that a good kiss was one in which they initiated the tongue contact. Women preferred less tongue contact with short-term partners, and more with long-term partners. Although men generally felt the same, they still overwhelmingly preferred more tongue contact than women with a short-term partner. This is tied into the hormones exchanged through saliva, but biology aside, men are less likely to spread their seed if they attack their date tongue first.

The Earth-shattering conclusions continue. It was revealed that men are much more likely to jump in the sack with someone they considered a poor kisser, and females were much less likely to kiss someone they knew only wanted sex from them.

Once in a relationship, the trend of women more highly valuing kissing continues. Girlfriends and wives placed great importance on kissing throughout the relationship, but spoken-for males rated kissing as not important in a long-term relationship. Women even reported a greater jealously than men did over a partner kissing someone else, viewing it as a more emotional (than sexual) betrayal.

Don't lose all faith in those sex-hungry men, though. There is evidence that on some level, men crave the same emotional connection as women—they just might not be conscious of it. Sex worker and advocate for legal brothels, Bethany St. James, has appeared on television and written a column for *The Huffington Post* to talk about the rise of the "Girlfriend Experience," or GFE. St. James and some of the other legal prostitutes of Nevada have seen a remarkable increase in requests that are less the "Porn Star Experience" and more the GFE. The prostitute *may* engage in sex with a client, but the emphasis is on talking, cuddling, and of course, kissing.

"Kissing and tenderness has never been at such an all-time premium," St. James remarks. The way to kiss, reactions to a kiss, and importance of kissing are divided by gender, but despite what the media tells men, they crave emotional connection as well—they just are less likely than women to seek it through a smooch alone.

# Dealing with a Breakup

## You need to be kinder to yourself

You're adjusting to your new status as "single." You're blasting some good breakup tunes, and going out on the town with your buddies and meeting people. And you do want to learn from this experience, so you're thinking really hard about what you might have done wrong. Really hard. You're not afraid to go in deep on this one. You're going to figure out how to do it better next time. Right now you're doing some soul-searching . . . and analyzing.

But if you don't show yourself compassion, you will take longer to feel better and move on.

**HOW TO DO IT RIGHT**
## Treat yourself as you would want others to treat you

Love yourself and "recognize the common humanity in the experience," says researcher David Sbarra. This is called "self-compassion," and people who express feelings of loving themselves and recognizing they're not alone and other people have felt what they feel have more resilience when dealing with a breakup.

You know how frustrating it is when you're freaked out and someone tells you to "relax"? That's part of the problem with learning self-compassion after a breakup. Anxiety will keep you away from breaking through to being kind and loving with yourself, but you can't *force* yourself away from the anxiety, and you certainly can't beat yourself up further. Personality plays a big part in how you react, and women tend to handle it with more self-compassion than men.

To help yourself be kinder to *you* after a breakup, keep your experience in perspective. Many people have experienced a painful and difficult breakup, and you're not alone. A breakup is part of the human experience, and realizing you're a part of a collective can help shift your perception to a healthier place. Dr. Sbarra also recommends remaining mindful, and in the present. Notice when you feel anger or jealousy, and accept and release it—don't judge it, even if you struggle with releasing it.

Self-compassion is different from self-esteem. Self-esteem often falters when we are less-than-perfect, and dives into depression and anxiety. Self-compassion recognizes that humans are flawed and our "failures" are part of our humanity and tie us into the greater whole of the human experience. Self-compassion is about failing, and giving yourself a hug. Literally. Self-compassion expert Kristin Neff recommends hugging yourself, and she doesn't care how ridiculous you think that is. You can start off by crossing your arms over your chest and giving yourself a subtle hug. Hugging yourself releases oxytocin, which ups your feelings of safety and calmness. "When we soothe our own pain, we are tapping into the mammalian care-giving system," Dr. Neff advises.

Meditation will help keep you mindful, and in the moment instead of mooning over the past; guided meditations are available free online on sites like

YouTube.com, and Nass's site *www.self-compassion.org* offers a free online meditation specifically for improving self-compassion.

Nine months after a divorce, all the subjects in Sbarra's study felt better than they did when the break-ups were fresh. So the good news is, it does get better. But it will get better faster and you will be more resilient if you can be kind and loving to yourself. Go ahead and give yourself a hug . . . no one needs to know you did and you will still get a boost!

# Handling Romantic Jealousy

It's not only for people with poor self-esteem or uncertain relationships, but it has a good shot of destroying your relationship, and is more about control than you realize

Feeling jealousy in a romantic relationship may be unavoidable. It comes in many forms, but most people think that jealousy is either a symptom of poor self-esteem or they are just being smart, vigilant, and guarding their relationships. And a billion studies have shown men really only think of the sexual aspect, and women the emotional. So you're either going to be the type to stuff it all down and ignore it, or be really raw and honest about your emotions—and totally check your partner's texts the first second her phone is left undetected. Better safe than sorry.

As it turns out, *even with healthy self-esteem*, romantic jealousy is a natural part of our wiring, but acting on suspicion will probably kill your relationship.

## HOW TO DO IT RIGHT

### Keep the green-eyed monster at bay

Don't hide your feelings in the assumption jealousy is only for people with low self-esteem. But if you're getting to the point of checking your partner's personal correspondence out of jealousy, you have some 'splaining to do. Whatever jealousy you feel *or* don't feel often comes down to control issues.

In *Psychology Today*, Hara Estroff Marano remarked on jealousy: "Ironic that an impulse that arises from love can so easily destroy it." Jealousy has its evolutionary purpose, alerting us to any threats to the bonds of our romantic relationships. In some weird ways, jealousy can be a positive thing. A report by psychologist David Buss found that 40 percent of women use a purposeful provocation of jealousy to "test" their mates via reaction, and psychologically, it is accurate that showing *some* jealousy is an indication that the relationship is "safe." If your partner doesn't care enough to feel jealousy at all, it's indicative of an overall sense of romantic apathy.

Romantic jealousy has long been associated with low self-esteem. Although people with low self-esteem *are* likely to express jealousy, they can also go to the opposite end of the spectrum and express *none*, because they just feel lucky to have a partner and don't want to rock the boat. Most of it boils down to control issues. When we feel a third party is threatening our relationship beyond our control, we feel jealousy. For low-self esteem people who don't feel "worthy" of feeling jealousy, not rocking the boat with the "negative" feeling may be the only thing they feel they can control.

Others with low self-esteem get jealous quickly, because they feel their partners are out of their league and thus, losing them to a rival is probably imminent. Often, this is the person who begins trying to control the relationship. He attempts to keep constant tabs on his partner's whereabouts, checks his partner's e-mails and texts, and makes accusations. This is the point of almost no return. If the relationship is new, the majority of partners ditch out, as insecurity is not hot. If the relationship is worth fighting for, couples therapy can help a person overcome her romantic jealousy, but only if she is able to be honest about it, face it, and work on it.

Often romantic jealousy comes from observing adults when we were children. For example, if a boy's mother is unfaithful to his father, the boy might seek to heal that childhood wound as an adult by constantly accusing his mate of infidelity. Each times she proves her innocence, the innocence itself feels healing to the childhood wound. Just as it sounds, this takes professional help to heal, but it is completely treatable when a person is ready to tackle it.

When we feel our relationships are out of our control, our behaviors are more likely to get out of control too, because often an element of "self"—or maybe the whole sense of self—is tied into our romantic relationships. This happens in more benign ways, like posting something embarrassing on an ex's Facebook wall, or in totally baffling creepster ways, like the astronaut-in-training who drove nonstop in a diaper to kidnap her romantic rival. By actually recognizing we are struggling with *control* (yes, anger and sadness too, but most people miss the control part), we can start to rein ourselves in and give our sense of self back to . . . ourselves.

If your partner is trying to control you through jealousy, red alert! And if someone displays zero jealousy whatsoever, he may just be "playing it cool," or may think quite honestly you are way too cool for him and he's just gonna keep quiet and hang on as long as possible.

# "Working On" Your Relationship

## The "failure" of a relationship just might be a success for you both

You know certain people you might have to just walk away from in a relationship. A person with a substance problem, or other addiction, like gambling, in which he constantly neglects your needs, putting the addiction first. A violent person, an unstable person, an angry person—you know it's okay to walk away from relationships with these kinds of people. But what about when nothing dramatic is "wrong" . . . but it's just not right? Don't you just need to work harder to see eye to eye and appreciate each other?

But if you and your partner have developed different value systems, it may be time to separate.

## Know when to fold 'em

Recognize if your value system—or your partner's—has significantly changed throughout the course of the relationship. For example, if years ago you loved her cutthroat, uber-successful approach to her business, but now you find you value kindness and philanthropy more, that may be driving you apart—and it may be a difference in core values in which no one is "wrong" or "right," but two people have significantly different needs.

Some people are academic and love intellectual discussions, sharing books, and ruminating over classical philosophy. This intellectual might fall in love with a quirky visual artist who can't sit still long enough to read a whole chapter, but for years, the difference doesn't matter. Over time, the intellectual may grow frustrated and lose respect for his flighty partner. The artist may lose respect for the intellectual's stuffiness and lack of emotional freedom. It doesn't mean a mismatched pair is doomed to failure. It means if, over time, your personal value system shifts and grows, and something you once valued but didn't need becomes an emotional need that's going unfulfilled—you may be better off if you both move on.

Having differences isn't what breaks a relationship—difference is a cure for boredom, and can keep things interesting and prevent partners from taking each other for granted. But when the difference becomes a core goal or value, you might feel like your partner isn't able to "see" the real you, and therefore, isn't loving the *real* you. In this way, your base need in a romantic relationship is going unmet in what psychologists might call a "soft" way. There's no "hard" reason like addiction, abuse, or even infidelity. But it's often the reason why people who marry young have such high divorce rates, because as they develop a stronger sense of self, they may find they no longer "match" their values to those of their partners.

In some cases, the old, "it's not you, it's me" is extremely accurate: You chose a partner before you knew what you really wanted. Your belief systems, lifestyle, choices, and what you hold most sacred might all have changed, grown, and no longer fit with your partner's changing and growing self. It's not a failure of the relationship, it's just the way humans emotionally and spiritually develop.

Pretty much all psychologists agree no long-term romantic relationship is going to feel right all the time. In fact, it's going to feel really wrong at some point. Boston family therapist Terrence Real theorizes that everyone in a long-term relationship will have a moment of certainty that they chose the wrong partner. It's normal, and every relationship takes work. But when you find the work isn't working . . . maybe your core values have changed.

# Texting Your Partner

## Of course, it is often misused, but science has found texting can actually be romantic and improve your relationship

The perils of texting. According to a poll by Recombu. com published in *The Huffington Post*, one in ten people has been dumped via text message. And that's nothing compared to the public scandal when someone is caught inappropriately "sexting" and the pics of his private parts go public. Careers and reputations are easily smashed via text these days. And isn't text-only a huge communication failure?

Yes, text alone conveys very little, but it turns out that the very little that *does* get through can mean a whole lot to your partner.

## HOW TO DO IT RIGHT

## Be *intelextually* responsible

It's not just for teenagers—sending a romantic text to your partner helps keep you connected emotionally. In fact, texting can be an emotional bridge to keep you connected during your busy days. It may be impossible (and not practical) to place a phone call, but it's easy to fire off a romantic, humorous, or cute personal message to your partner, which keeps up the connection even while you're apart.

Every bad notion you have about texting is probably true. It leads to miscommunication; it can be "used" for confrontation (and dumping); it is incredibly dangerous while driving; and any naked pictures you send might end up being seen by someone you really, really, didn't want to see them. But when used for light, positive messages between couples, it actually strengthens the bond.

Part of the appeal is just knowing your partner is thinking about you. Even a quick "I <3 u" may seem silly, but it is likely to raise the recipient's mood. Sending a <3 way too immature for you? Send a compliment, a funny observation about your day, or a veiled sexual innuendo. They all work to help reinforce that invisible bridge of connection between couples as they carry on with their separate lives.

Dr. Adrian Aguilera, a psychologist at UC Berkeley, discovered texting his patients about positive interactions improved their moods, even when simply receiving automated texts. "My life is so crazy, I need a reminder to think about how I feel," a patient of Aguilera's told *Science Daily*. The psychological value of texts still has much to be studied, but from these initial findings it's fairly obvious that positive texts lift mood. People are so easily distracted by *everything*, they may even get "distracted" from feeling loved and connected. Just as Aguilera's automated texts helped center his patients, romantic texts from a partner remind you that you are loved, right in that second, even though there was no discernible, physical "source" of love around you.

Don't get boring with your texts, keep an edge of raciness and humor. Picture mails don't have to be mundane or explicit . . . they can be somewhere in a happy medium. A 2011 study by Dr. Sarah Coyne, et al. found the happiest couples were those whose number one reason for texting was "expressing affection." Although texts were used most frequently by people aged seventeen to twenty-four, it was a remarkably minor drop-off between age groups, with adults twenty-five to forty texting only slightly less than their counterparts, and ages forty-one to fifty also texting only slightly less than the younger demographic. Even with variables such as age and relationship status accounted for, Coyne's study found "higher relationship satisfaction predicted more media use to express affection."

You don't have to use hearts and endless goofy emoticons, but if you don't already, try an affection-for-no-reason text with your partner. Anything positive to reinforce that your partner is thought of during your busy days will help strengthen your bond.

# Protecting Yourself Against STDs

## Using protection wrong, using the wrong kind of protection, and thinking age itself is some kind of protection are all hugely common mistakes

The last thing you want to think about on a date is sexually transmitted diseases. In the excitement of finding a new partner, whether for a relationship or just right now, there's a sort of high you don't want to dampen with downer thoughts of disease. Besides, you're responsible! You're totally going to use a condom! What the hell—condom, spermicide, you have an entire arsenal of protection available at the nearest drugstore.

Well, if you actually follow through with that intention, you have about a 50 percent chance of still doing it wrong.

## HOW TO DO IT RIGHT

### Handle with care—no matter what your age

Proper condom use is the somewhat annoyingly prim answer, but it's true. You're totally sure you're using condoms right, but most people actually don't. They put them on too snugly (not leaving any room at the tip), or too quickly, trapping air inside which leads to popping, or too messily, contaminating both sides of the condom before it's been unrolled. And one of the more dangerous and frequent choices, they are removed during sex and disposed of altogether . . . while the sex continues unprotected, leaving no freaking point to using a condom in the first place, except maybe the illusion of safety.

Multiple studies on protection keep finding the same themes on the errors people make in protection while putting the "doing it" in doing it wrong:

- Improper condom use. Condoms are the frontline of sexually transmitted disease prevention, but the Kinsey Institute reports on tons of problems people have with condom use, including 74.5 percent of men and 82.7 percent of women not checking for visible damage to the condom before using it. So the majority of people are actually failing one of the "easiest" steps. (In retrospect, pun completely intended.)

- Teens are more likely to use condoms than their grandfathers. Maybe you haven't heard, but sexually transmitted disease is on the rise in *nursing homes*. And it's not just the elderly—the age at which the condom-using demographic of sexually active people drops off is forty-five. Hormonal changes in post-menopausal women mean that pregnancy is no longer a worry, but it also means these women are more vulnerable to disease. Some doctors theorize older people feel like "they made it this far" safe and thus, the risk isn't as dire as presented. It totally is, so knock it off, older-than-forty-fivers. Next time you hear a politician or talk-radio windbag talking about youth endangered by sex, it would be nice if someone could point out to him that *his* age group is actually behaving the riskiest.

- Don't use spermicide for protection. Sure, it kills sperm, but it doesn't kill diseases, and many well-intentioned men and women are using it with such hopes. In reality, it makes people *more* vulnerable to disease, thanks to its irritating properties, which the Centers for Disease Control and Prevention (CDC) describes as "disruption of the genital epithelium." Ouch. Although it's a great tool for preventing pregnancy (especially for women who can't tolerate hormonal birth control), many people still don't realize it won't help them stay disease-free. Some initial studies found spermicide might reduce HIV risk by 30 percent, but those and other studies underway are actually examining antimicrobials that also happen to be spermicidal, not the Nonoxynol-9 that's available in the United States.

Hey, it could be worse—condoms used to be made of tortoiseshell, animal horn, animal intestines, and other rough, unpleasant, and overall disgusting materials. As far as protection goes, the modern age is pretty lucky gettin' lucky.

# Online Dating

## Those magical "matching algorithms" don't work as well as they should, because we don't understand what we actually want

Online dating time means it's time to fill out those profiles, questionnaires, and get some flattering snapshots taken of yourself. Whether you're looking for a hookup or a marriage, online is your best bet, because it's totally scientific. You put in tons of information, and it's compared to other people's information, and a computer matches you up way better than you ever could have done just meeting strangers in the real world or through awkward recommendations from relatives.

And that would be somewhat true, except what people think and say they want tends to not be want they *really* want.

**HOW TO DO IT RIGHT**

## Get by with a little help from your friends

Get real honest with yourself, as Los Angeles–based psychologist Dr. Sinead Flanagan likes to say. The number one truth-intentioned lie is based in physical attraction. People generally think they care less about someone being hot and sexy than they actually do.

They don't want to date the troll under the bridge, but they don't demand a princess, either. And they probably really think that's true . . . but it's not.

Northwestern University's Eli Finkel and Paul Eastwick coauthored a study on the science of online dating, and found the "science" element to be lacking—there are no hard data or peer-reviewed studies when it comes to a specific site's algorithm for matchmaking. Unlike eHarmony, who owns their (specific, top-secret) formula, this study of what people say they want and what they reveal they want under further psychological study are two different things.

"If a person tells me, for example, that she doesn't care about how attractive a guy is, our research suggests that her claim isn't worth all that much," Eastwick explains. It's not that people are liars (well, some are, obviously) but we have "unconscious preferences."

One way to deal with those preferences is to get help from people who know you well. One successful online dater told *PC World* he had two friends look over his answers to eHarmony's questions to help him become aware of any preferences. Science has yet to show if there are any hard numbers behind trying to be honest with the matching algorithm, because the sites don't release their data. The research from Finkel and Eastwick's study suspects the whole "algorithm" system is more like a placebo.

Finkel advises for the best results, don't spend too much time purely online—use online to make real-world dates, and get out and meet people to find out if you "click" or not. Interaction and conflict management are two of the biggest ways to judge if a relationship will work, and it's impossible to find those things out online. Some factors of the oh-so-important physical attraction, like voice, mannerisms, and even smell, are also impossible to determine online.

What you can find online is a starting point for meeting people. Second only to meeting through friends and family, dating sites are popular for a reason. The science may be soft—or nonexistent—but it can be a springboard to reality.

# Speed Dating

## Don't discount it in favor of online dating only, and don't just sit there, be the one who rotates!

Speed dating, do people still do that? Well, it gives you the benefit of avoiding misleading profile pictures and the common lies about physical descriptions, of which a whopping 80 percent of people online are guilty. Plus it was pretty hilarious in *The 40-Year-Old Virgin*. So, okay, you'll go, if you can be the one who rotates seat to seat, so you can run if someone is just awful.

But if you really want to meet a person you're attracted to, log off your profile and approach someone.

### HOW TO DO IT RIGHT

## Don't dismiss it in favor of only finding potential dates online, which feels "easier," because it is—but not in a good way

Some psychologists theorize browsing for dates online gives us a "browsing a catalogue" feeling. We may think we are attracted based on the picture, but there's no substitute for face-to-face interaction because we are social creatures by nature. It's no shock that people don't find cybersex a reasonable replacement for real sex, or that humans long to have romantic interactions with other actual humans, not digital representatives of them.

One of the problems with speed dating is that the organizers often have the rotation backwards. It seems logical to have the women remain seated and the men rotating the approach, as women tend to have purses and more "stuff" with them, plus it goes along with the stereotype of the male should approach the female. But when researchers studied speed dating, they found that when women approached men, they felt more confident and were more likely to select more potential dates. Statistically, women at speed dating events are choosier than men, so if speed dating companies were to reverse their standard and have women approach men, they would produce more matches. If you've decided to take the plunge and try speed dating, ask the company who approaches whom. If the woman approaches you, she'll find you more attractive, and if you are the female, you'll feel more confident when approaching than being approached.

Dr. Scott Barry Kaufman found that the chances of speed dating leading to a sexual hookup was 6 percent, and the chances of a relationship forming were 4 percent. He estimated it would take about seventy-five hours of speed dating to find a great match, and cost about $1,000 in speed dating service fees. So apparently one *can* put a price on finding love. Price of physical love only statistically may be cheaper, and your mileage may vary.

# HOME
# AND AUTO

# Removing Stains from Clothing

## Using a stain stick or chlorine bleach, and being impatient

Pit stains on your white T-shirt? Drop it in the wash with a little bleach, and it's good as—Hey wait! Is the stain even darker now? Yes, it is. Red wine on your shirt? You apply stain stick and drop the shirt straight in the wash . . . and then when it's done, you have slightly less red wine on your shirt. Ink stain on your jeans? You're not messing around, so you get an industrial-strength stain remover from the hardware store and pour it on. Well, now there's no more stain, but there's a weird pale spot on your jeans. It's not the stain remover, it's you.

HOW TO DO IT RIGHT

## Use your products wisely

The main problem with the ol' standbys of stain sticks and bleach for stain removal is that not all stains are created equal, and what removes a stain from some fabrics will destroy another fabric, even though the fabrics might feel or look the same. It would be a hard sell for some stain sticks to come with honest descriptions like, "For protein stains on cotton only!" or "For oil stains only!" Or how about if a product admitted "All fabric bleach: not actually for all fabrics"?

The truth is, stain removal is basic chemistry. It involves acids, bases, pH balance, and organic and synthetic materials. That's why dry cleaning is an entire profession. A few tough stains will require professional help, but you can maximize what you're able to achieve at home by ignoring what products *say* they do, and instead using them to their best purpose.

In *Betty's Book of Laundry Secrets*, authors Betty Faust and Maria Rodale eschew stain sticks, advising: "A lot of those stain-removing products you can buy at grocery stores leave spots on clothes." The authors found the best stain removal products are a bar of Ivory soap and a scrub brush. The scrub brush helps break up the stain with elbow grease instead of chemicals, and the Ivory is effective because of its neutral pH balance. Make sure you get the plain white bar with no added colors, fragrances, or moisturizers. The simple steps are to soak the fabric in water and rub the Ivory bar directly onto the stain, and then rinse. If the stain remains, do it again but this time, use the scrub brush and then soak for half an hour in cold water, and then rinse.

For those pit stains on a white T-shirt, it seems obvious to wash them with bleach, but the chemistry of sweat and bleach results in just darkening the spot. Try the neutral bar soap, and dry in direct sunlight to provide a natural bleaching that is sweat-compatible. Your dryer's heat may actually worsen and set the stains.

For red wine stains, you can stop the stain from setting with white wine. While the stain is still fresh, apply (but don't rub!) some salt, give it a few minutes to sink in, and rinse in *warm* water. For white wine, one part glycerin mixed with two parts water rubbed in before a regular wash should remove the problem.

How about the ink stain on jeans? Jeans are generally made of cotton, which can stand a little more treatment than silk, wool, or some synthetics. Use a dry cloth to dab on some rubbing alcohol, then apply some detergent, and then wash. This is where the other secret to stain removal comes in: patience. Even though those products may advertise "instant," the truth is, a deep stain requires time for the agents to break up the bond, and it may take several rounds of work to remove.

It's highly unlikely Guns N' Roses was thinking of laundry when they wrote the song "Patience," but go ahead and hum it when you're on your third round with the same stain as it ever-so-slowly lightens. Even rock stars don't rock pit stains.

# Using WD-40

## Thinking it's a lubricant

Ah, WD-40, much like our friend duct tape, it's good for everything. You spray it on your tools, your bike chain, your front door lock, your hunting rifle, and anything that squeaks— including your neighbor's dog, which said neighbor is still pretty pissed about. If only the whole world were covered in WD-40, everything would run smoothly.

Except no, because you're doing it wrong.

## HOW TO DO IT RIGHT

## Don't overlook the lube

WD-40 has many functions, and one of them is lubrication, but it's not technically a true lubricant. "WD" stands for "Water Displacement" and 40 means the fortieth try, so the name is straight from the lab in the 1950s. But a water displacement agent is just a little different from a lubricant, so slowly back away from the spray can.

WD-40 is a great cleaner and rust preventer, but only a partial lubricant. For best results on items that need true lubrication, clean with WD-40 and follow with a lubricant.

Its application to firearms is probably WD-40's most controversial use. Although it *can* be used on them, gun experts certainly don't find it optimal. An article on *TheGunZone.com* suggests "WD-40 tends to gum and turn into a varnish with time." Other firearms experts have cited similar problems, such as a "waxy" finish after drying.

The bicycle chain is another hot topic. I know you're probably thinking that your dad put it on your bike all the time when you were a kid, and it was fine. It can be "fine," but most of its power comes from cleaning, not proper lubrication. Sporting goods store REI states on its website that it doesn't recommend WD-40 for bike chains, as "it will clean the chain all right but it will not lubricate." *Boys' Life* magazine agreed and recommends Teflon for bike chain lubrication.

At this point, you're probably catching on to the "not a true lubricant" theme, but WD-40 is also not best for hinges. It will clean them and free up rusted parts, but to stop squeaking, use a silicon lubricant.

Looks like your high school shop teacher was right: Use the right tool for the right job. But even he probably used probably used WD-40 as a lubricant.

# Training Your Dog

**HOW YOU'RE DOING IT WRONG**

## Using the popular "alpha dog" aggression-submission behavior model

Dogs are pack animals, descended from wolves. Studies have shown wolf packs have "alpha wolves" that run the pack, so the best way to control your dog's behavior is to *become* the alpha yourself. Wrestle that li'l doggie to the ground—carefully!—but show him who the alpha is, and you'll be the head of your twosome wolf pack.

Except those studies took place in the 1940s, and as it turns out, missed crucial information.

**HOW TO DO IT RIGHT**

## Pawsitive Pups

The most famous trainer utilizing the alpha dog theory is Cesar Millan, star of National Geographic Channel's hit show, *Dog Whisperer with Cesar Millan*. Millan's success is appealing, and his skill with and love of dogs is indisputable, but as the show cautions: "do not try this at home." One man's incredibly specialized skill set unfortunately does not relate to the general public. The good news is, there are several successful methods you can employ, as well as taking a few of Millan's more gentle lessons.

Positive reinforcement is a more successful form of training, in which the dog isn't punished for bad behavior, but shown a better way to act and rewarded for positive behavior. Victoria Stilwell is one of the world's most famous dog trainers and uses positive reinforcement, as seen on her Animal Planet show *It's Me or the Dog!* which is aired in more than forty countries. Science stands behind Stilwell's methods, proving the old wolf studies as flawed, as well as not correlating to dogs. (In fact one of the original wolf researchers has been trying to correct the erroneous alpha wolf myth for years, as the wolves in his research were not from the wild or related in a natural family structure.) Researchers have found dogs respond to aggression-based training because they are afraid, and view their trainer (and caretakers) as a predator.

A happy dog is a much healthier dog, so positivity goes a long way. When you have a dog that is acting out, he first needs to go to the vet, as health problems are a common cause of aggression or another behavioral problems in dogs. Stilwell spoke out with the American Veterinary Medical Association (AVMA) to clarify that although aggression may seem like a display of confidence in a dog, it's actually the opposite. An aggressive dog is a scared, insecure dog, and adding more fear-based actions will only keep the animal in a fear state. To heal the problem, you must find the root of the dog's problem. If the vet rules out physical problems, the dog could be reacting to anything from trauma to simply not having enough exposure to new people and environments.

Like a human child, dogs take their confidence and safety cues from their parents—in this case, human "parent" or caretaker. If your dog has been aggressive, being nervous when you take him out will "tell" him it's not safe, and the aggression will continue. By the time your dog is acting aggressively, it's too late to correct the behavior—the dog is now too emotional to learn. Whether you try to love it or use a choke collar, modern research indicates the dog isn't really able to "learn" right in that heated moment. Instead, you need to be aware of your dog's triggers, and act *before* the trouble begins. When addressing the AVMA, Stilwell discussed the common problem of trying to walk your problematic dog, yet the dog becomes aggressive when someone approaches. She advises that when you see a person start to approach, making your dog *think* and use his brain will distract him from getting emotional and aggressive. To make him think, teach him to sit and look at you, or throw a treat on the ground in a "finding" game, and praise him as he learns. As this continues, the dog slowly associates a person approaching with something good happening to him, and his behavior modifies to be positive. Stilwell has successfully used this method to turn countless growlers into playful pups as they are approached.

Use your body language to give your dog cues. Dogs want your attention, so when they are naughty, ignoring them is more successful than punishment. When your dog jumps up on your visitor, your inclination might be to reprimand, but you'll have more success if you ignore the dog, with your arms crossed and your gaze distant, as if the dog were not even in the room. Trainer and *Dog Sense* author John Bradshaw notes that "withdrawing" sends a signal to your dog louder than a million dog whistles.

With positive-based training easily accessible online and on television, it's becoming easier than ever to move forward with canine science in your own home. Leave those antiquated notions of captive wolf behavior (not literally) to the dogs.

# Feeding Your Cat

## Stop leaving a bowl of dry food out—cats weren't meant to consume carbohydrates all day!

Despite the fact that they obviously hate you and occasionally plot your murder, cats are usually far simpler pets to care for than dogs. It's easier to scoop the litter any time that's convenient for you than to take the animal for a walk, and cats are pretty independent, so leave a few toys out and let 'em do their own thing. Just leave a bowl in the corner for water, and one for food, and fill it up with kibble every few days. Your vet tells you dry food also helps keep the cat's teeth clean.

Alert! If your vet is advocating a dry food diet, he hasn't checked in with the latest research.

## HOW TO DO IT RIGHT

## Take the plunge into wet food

Feed your cat wet, canned food. Or a homemade diet, but that's not even practical or reasonable for most humans, never mind their pets. Vets used to advocate the super-easy dry food method, citing it leaves the teeth cleaner. Vet tech Amanda Wellman cites more recent research findings that "saying eating dry food cleans cats' teeth is like saying eating potato chips cleans humans' teeth."

If you've ever had an indoor and outdoor cat, you probably already know what a cat's "natural" diet consists of—birds, lizards, mice, insects, and other gross things they can feast on like they totally weren't *just the cutest widdle furball* two seconds ago. Our bloodthirsty beloveds are obligatory carnivores—they need meat to live. (Run far from anyone who tells you it's possible for cats to be vegetarian! Dogs might get by that way, but cats *cannot*.) Whatever a wild cat would be able to catch varies daily, so cats are naturally built to require variety in their diet.

Protein is the key for our cuddly, super-soft, terrorizing hunters. Dry food contains starch-based carbohydrates, which make up 35 to 50 percent of the food. Holy fat cat! Even if you manage to get one of the fancier "grain free" dry foods, it's still going to be a whopping 20 percent carbs. Much of this has to do with how the food is produced: under high heat, in which most proteins are damaged. Cereal grains are tougher, cheaper, and provide calories, but are not part of the cat's natural diet. The results of the dry food diet can be dehydration, constipation, and bowel disease. The obesity resulting from the carb-happy diet can cause kidney failure, diabetes, and problems for the liver function and joints.

For a significantly long time in veterinary history, dry food was considered to clean cats' teeth, but new research proves that is not true. If your vet is advocating a dry food diet to keep the precious kitty's razor-sharp fangs clean, it doesn't mean she has bad intentions, it just means she's lagging on her research (which, granted, isn't all that impressive).

Dry food can be useful, but it should never make up more than 50 percent of the cat's diet—100 percent wet food is the ideal. Choose cat food like you would human food—look for natural brands, with recognizable ingredients and high protein. The best foods will not be available in the grocery store—you'll have to go to a pet store, or a natural foods store with a pets section. It is more expensive, but often proves to be *less* expensive over time as it results in a healthier animal with fewer vet bills in the long run.

Many cats have a dry food addiction, and switching them over to wet food will take a little time. Or maybe he is just being a cat, and being finicky. Veterinarian Jean Hofve recommends leaving dry food out for one hour in the morning and one hour in the evening, to slowly get kitty weaned off of it. Your cat may have a dry food addiction, or it may simply not want to try something new, so as its dry food option is slowly removed, so shall Princess PickyPants slowly consider trying that wet food she knows you're totally trying to kill her with.

# Taking Care of Your Lawn

**HOW YOU'RE DOING IT WRONG**

## Cutting it too low and overwatering it

Even if you don't have the lawn love of Texan cartoon character Hank Hill, you still probably like to see your lawn looking green. So what are the basics? Sunlight, water, and keep it mowed, right? Yes, but most people are doing too much of the second and third on that list. And if it were possible for you to make the sun stay out longer, you would probably be three for three.

**HOW TO DO IT RIGHT**

## Let the grass do its thing

Never cut the grass lower than one-third of the blade height, and don't overwater. Landscaping expert Griffin Bartlett with Rye Beach Landscaping of New Hampshire says the most common things he sees are lawns "burnt" from low mowing and drowning flowers from overzealous watering. Grass height of about 3 inches is ideal, and in most cases it will need to be mowed about once a week. For many people, the temptation is just to cut the grass down as low as possible to give them as much time as possible between mows, but that doesn't leave enough moisture-retaining leaf to keep the grass healthy. Also, when you decrease the surface area of the grass, there's less photosynthesis, which means the grass is less healthy and less green.

Mowing your grass too closely is called "scalping." In cases where the root system of the grass is damaged by close cutting, weeds can move in. Some people scalp their lawns in hopes of removing weeds, but weeds need to be pulled (or chemically destroyed), whereas grass is more delicate, so the scalping only exacerbates the weed problem.

Lawns only need 1 to 1.5 inches of water a week, so most people running their sprinklers are overwatering. Many sprinklers are automated and run regardless of rainfall. If you're not living in a drought-prone area, you may even have seen automatic sprinklers showering away obliviously during a rainstorm.

Roots seek moisture, so overwatered lawns are bound to have root problems, as the roots aren't stretching and growing properly. It's best to water between 3:00 A.M. and 6:00 A.M., mimicking dew. If that's not possible (or just insane), water as early as possible. Watering once or twice a week is better than watering a small amount every day. In many climates, that also mimics nature's pattern, and allows roots to grow more deeply. When watered every day, they don't need to stretch. You might say they get downright lazy.

If you have flowers in your yard, they are in danger over being overwatered as well. When the soil is damp, the flowers don't need more water. Overwatering will not allow the roots to "breathe," and the suffocated plants will look much like those that are thirsty—wilted, yellowed, with no new growth. If you see greenish soil, that may be algae, which sure sounds like you're trying to turn your flowerbed into a pond.

It's not easy being green . . . but it's not always that hard, either. With a little luck in terms of climate and moderation in your watering and cutting habits, that purdy lawn can be yours. Suck it, annoying neighbor!

# Resources

Amar, Moty; Ariely, Dan; Ayal, Shahar; Cryder, Cynthia E.; Rick, Scott I. "Winning the Battle but Losing the War: The Psychology of Debt Management." *Journal of Marketing Research*, 48 (Special Issue), S38–S50, 2011.

The American Academy of Dermatology. (*www.aad.org*)

The American Academy of Otolaryngology. "Fact Sheet: Common Problems That Can Affect Your Voice." (*www.entnet.org/HealthInformation/commonvoiceproblems.cfm*)

Ancowitz, Nancy. "Self-Promotion for Introverts: How to Negotiate with the Terminator." *Psychology Today*, January 3, 2011. (*www.psychologytoday.com*)

Anwar, Yasmin. " 'Uok?' Text Messages Can Soothe the Disconnected Soul." *Science Daily*, April 10, 2012. (*www.sciencedaily.com*)

Anyaso, Hilary Hurd. "Do You Really Know What You Want in a Partner?" *www.northwestern.edu*, November 14, 2011.

Arthur, Meredith; Slatkin, Eric; Smith, Blake. "How to Tap a Keg with JD Beebe." *Chow*, January 8, 2009. (*www.chow.com*)

Arthur, Meredith; Smith, Blake; Szymanowski, Mathew. "How to (Properly) Eat Sushi with Trevor Corson." *Chow*, October 19, 2010. (*www.chow.com*)

Aubrey, Allison. "Coffee: A Little Really Does Go a Long Way." *National Public Radio*, "Morning Edition," September 28, 2006. (*www.npr.org*)

Ayres, Janelle S.; Schneider, David S. "The Role of Anorexia in Resistance and Tolerance to Infections in Drosophila." *PLoS Biology*, July 14, 2009. (*www.plosbiology.org*)

Barbour, Matthew. "Seven Daily Sins: Shower Every Day? Rinse After Brushing Teeth? These 'Healthy' Habits Could Be Devilishly Bad for You." *MailOnline*, April 27, 2011. (*www.dailymail.co.uk*)

Barrecca, Regina, PhD. "Snow White Doesn't Live Here Anymore: Sweet Revenge." *Psychology Today*, January 1, 2010. (*www.psychologytoday.com*)

Bartlett, Griffin. Personal interview, April 2012. (*http://ryebeachlandscaping.com*)

Baume, Matthew. Personal interview, April 2012. (*http://mattbaume.com*)

Bedwell, Sarah-Jane. "Eat Like Me: Four Foods to Help You Stay Warm this Winter." *Self*, January 30, 2012. (*www.self.com*)

Bennett, Drake. "The Shaky Science of Online Dating." *Bloomberg BusinessWeek*, April 4, 2012. (*www.businessweek.com*)

Berard, Guy, MD. (*www.drguyberard.com*)

Bettcher, Jessica. Personal interview, April 2012. (*www.jessicabettcher.com*)

Beuke, Carl, PhD. "You're Hired: The Limits of Ambition." *Psychology Today*, December 9, 2011. (*www.psychologytoday.com*)

Bradshaw, John. *Dog Sense: How the New Science of Dog Behavior Can Make You a Better Friend to Your Pet.* (New York: Basic Books, 2011).

Branson, Richard. "On How to Avoid Common Startup Mistakes." *Entrepreneur*, November 15, 2011. (*www.entrepreneur.com*)

Brody, Jane E. "What Do You Lack? Probably Vitamin D." *The New York Times*, July 26, 2010. (*www.nytimes.com*)

Bryant, Cedric X. "Why Is the Concept of Spot Reduction Considered a Myth?" *ACE FitnessMatters,* January/February 2004. (*www.acefitness.org*)

Bryant, Charles W. "How Does Wool Keep You Warm Even When It's Wet?" (*www.adventure.howstuffworks.com*)

Burke, Kelly. "10 Lawn Care Mistakes." (*http://lawncare.about.com*)

Burkeman, Oliver. "This Column Will Change Your Life." *The Guardian*, August 1, 2008. (*www.guardian.co.uk*)

Bushman, Brad J. "Does Venting Anger Feed or Extinguish the Flame? Catharsis, Rumination, Distraction, Anger, and Aggressive Responding." *Personality and Social Psychology Bulletin*, Vol. 28, No. 6, pp. 724–731, June, 2002.

Bushman, Brad J., Baumeister, Roy F., and Phillips, Colleen M. "Do People Aggress to Improve Their Mood? Catharsis Beliefs, Affect Regulation Opportunity, and Aggressive Responding." *Journal of Personality and Social Psychology*, Vol. 81, No. 1, pp. 17–32, July 2001.

Buster, Jay. "Treadmill Desk: The $39 Treadmill Desk." (*www.treadmill-desk.com*)

California Academy of Sciences. "The History of Eating Utensils." (*http://research.calacademy.org*)

California State University, Northridge, Department of Police Services. "Stalking", January 6, 2011. (*www.admn.csun.edu*)

Carlsmith, Kevin M.; Wilson, Timothy D.; Gilbert, Daniel T. "The Paradoxical Consequences of Revenge." *Journal of Personality and Social Psychology*, Vol. 95, No. 6, pp. 1316–1324, December 2008. (*http://psycnet.apa.org*)

Centers for Disease Control and Prevention. (*www.cdc.gov*)

Chase, Raluca. Personal interview, April 2012. (*http://kalura.ro*)

Chavez, Amy. "Visitors' Deep-Seated Terror: Asian Toilets." *The Japan Times*, August 18, 2001. (*www.japantimes.co.jp*)

Child, Ben. "3D No Better than 2D and Gives Filmgoers Headaches, Claims Study." *The Guardian*, August 11, 2011. (*www.guardian.co.uk*)

Conley, Chris. "Quiz: What Do Facebook Quizzes Know About You?" ACLU of Northern California, June 11, 2009. (*www.aclunc.org*)

Corson, Trevor. (*www.trevorcorson.com*)

Coyne, Sarah M.; Stockdale, Laura; Busby, Dean; Iverson, Bethany; Grant, David M. " 'I luv u :)!': A Descriptive Study of the Media Use of Individuals in Romantic Relationships." *Family Relations*, April 2011, Volume 60, Issue 2, pp. 150–162.

Crane, Robert Morrison. "Social Distance and Loneliness as They Relate to Headphones Used with Portable Technology." Thesis (M.A.) Psychology, Counseling, Humboldt State University, 2005. (*http://humboldt-dspace.calstate.edu*)

Crannell, Kenneth C. *Voice and Articulation*. (Boston: Wadsworth Publishing, Fifth Edition, 2011).

Credit Union National Organization. (*www.cuna.org*)

Davies, Adam. "WD-40 Versus the World of Lubricants." *Popular Mechanics*, August 31, 2010. (*www.popularmechanics.com*)

Derr, Aaron. "How to Maintain Your Bike." *Boys' Life*, May 2008. (*http://boyslife.org*)

DiGregorio, Sarah. "Mind Your Manners: Eat with Your Hands." *The New York Times*, January 17, 2012. (*www.nytimes.com*)

Dillard, Mechele R. " 'Vocal fry' Sweeping Young Women's Speech Patterns, Study Suggests." *Huliq*, December 15, 2011. (*www.huliq.com*)

Dunbar, Dr. Ian. "Let's Just Be Humans Training Dogs" *Dog Star Daily*, August 31, 2010. (*www.dogstardaily.com*)

Dunn, Elizabeth W.; Gilbert, Daniel T.; Wilson, Timothy D. "If Money Doesn't Make You Happy, Then You Probably Aren't Spending It Right." *Journal of Consumer Psychology*, Vol. 21, pp. 115–125, 2011. (*www.sciencedirect.com*)

Duzak, Jim. "Can a Kiss Save Your Marriage?" *The Daily Buzz* "Headdrama," July 24, 2011. (*www.headdrama.com*)

Eastwick, Paul W.; Eagly, Alice H.; Finkle, Eli J.; Johnson, Sarah E. "Implicit and Explicit Preferences for Physical Attractiveness in a Romantic Partner: A Double Dissociation in Predictive Validity." *Journal of Personality and Social Psychology*, Vol. 101, No. 5, November 2011, pp. 993–110.

Ebert, Roger. "Why 3D Doesn't Work and Never Will. Case Closed." *The Chicago Sun-Times*, "Roger Ebert's Journal," January 23, 2011. (*http://blogs.suntimes.com/ebert*)

Ebron, Angela. "Is Jealousy Ruining Your Relationship? Consider These Stats." *The South Florida Sun-Sentinel*, *"Woman's Day,"* May 13, 2010.

Echlin, Helena. "Pointing the Finger at Finger Foods." *Chow*, September 27, 2007. (*www.chow.com*)

Eggleston, Emily. "Winter Wonders: The Science of Cold." *Scientific American*, December 26, 2011. (*http://blogs. scientificamerican.com*)

Epstein, Angela. "Nothing but the Tooth." *The Daily Mail*, May 6, 2012. (*www.dailymail.co.uk*)

Faust, Betty and Rodale, Maria. *Betty's Book of Laundry Secrets*, (Emmaus, PA: Rodale Books, 2001).

Feuerman, Simon Y. "My Mother, My Father, My Money: Thank You Usually Means Something Else." *Psychology Today*, April 13, 2009. (*www.psychologytoday.com*)

Field, George. *Chromatics*. (Nabu Press, August 30, 2011). (Reprint).

Firriolo, Rob. "Rust Preventatives for Firearms." *TheGunZone.com*, December 1, 2005.

Fishel, Anne K. PhD; Gorrindo, Tristan MD. "Improving Your Relationship: LUV LTRS and Other Digital Quickies." *Psychology Today*, April 30, 2011. (*www.psychologytoday.com*)

Flagg, Donna. *Surviving Dreaded Conversations: Talk Through Any Difficult Situation at Work.* (New York: The McGraw-Hill Companies, 2010).

Fussell, Nicola J.; Stollery, Brian T. "Between-Sex Differences in Romantic Jealousy: Substance or Spin? A Qualitative Analysis." *Evolutionary Psychology*, Vol. 10, No. 1, 2012, pp. 136–172. (*www.epjournal.net*)

Galloway, Ken. "Top 10: Rules of Sushi Etiquette." (*www.askmen.com*)

Gann, Carrie. "Sex Life of Older Adults and Rising STDs." *ABC News*, February 3, 2012. (*www.ABCNews.com*)

Giardina, Carolyn. "Debate Waging over 2D-to-3D Conversion." *The Hollywood Reporter*, April 4, 2010. (*www.hollywoodreporter.com*)

Goldman, Leslie. "Winning Isn't Everything: Why 'Everyone Gets a Turn' May Be Good for Little Kids." *Newsweek*, September 2, 2009.

Gollwitzer, Peter M.; Sheeran, Paschal; Michalski, Verena; Seifert, Andrea E. "When Intentions Go Public: Does Social Reality Widen the Intention-Behavior Gap?" *Psychological Science*, Vol. 20, No. 5, 2009. (*www.psych.nyu.edu*)

Gordon, Amie. "The Sleep Cycle: What's Really Going on While You're Catching Your Zzz's." *Berkeley Science Review*, September 14, 2011. (*http://sciencereview.berkeley.edu*)

Gordon, Claire. "Tipping in the Recession, Service Professionals Speak Out." *AOL Jobs*, October 4, 2011. (*http://jobs.aol.com*)

Gorlick, Adam. "Media Multitaskers Pay Mental Price, Stanford Study Shows." *Stanford Report*, August 24, 2009. (*http://news.stanford.edu*)

Goudarzi, Sara. "To Ease Back Pain, Don't Sit Up Straight." *MSNBC News*, November 28, 2006. (*www.msnbc.msn.com*)

Gray, Emma. "Relationships and Technology: Is Texting Ruining Romance?" *The Huffington Post*, January 20, 2012. (*www.huffingtonpost.com*)

Grifantini, Kristina. "Is 3D Bad for You?" *Technology Review* (published by Massachusetts Institute of Technology), April 5, 2010. (*www.technologyreview.com*)

Griffiths, Roland. "Caffeine Withdrawal Recognized as a Disorder." Johns Hopkins press release, September 29, 2004.

Groeneveld, Frank; Borsboom, Barry; van Amstel, Boy. "Over-sharing and Location Awareness." Center for Democracy & Technology, February 24, 2010. (*www.cdt.org*)

Gurley, Dr. Jan. "The Earbud Epidemic." *The San Francisco Chronicle* "SFGate," November 15, 2011. (*http://blog.sfgate.com/gurley*)

Gurley, Dr. Jan. "Wearing Headphones Not Just Bad For Your Ears." *The San Francisco Chronicle* "SFGate," January 18, 2012. (*http://blog.sfgate.com/gurley*)

Hall, Terri. "7 Ways to Stay Warm." *Care 2 Make a Difference*, December, 2008. (*www.care2.com*)

Hamady, Jennifer. "Finding Your Voice: You Are Not Your Talent." *Psychology Today*, February 10, 2012. (*www.psychologytoday.com*)

Hamilton, Ryan; Vohs, Kathleen; Sellier, Anne-Laure; Meyvis, Tom. "Being of Two Minds: Switching Mindsets Exhausts Self-Regulatory Resources." *Organizational Behavior and Human Decision Processes*, December 18, 2010.

Haselton, Martie G.; Buss, David M.; Oubaid, Viktor; Angleitner, Alois. "Sex, Lies, and Strategic Interference: The Psychology of Deception Between the Sexes." *Journal of Personality and Social Psychology*, Vol. 31, No. 1, January 2005, pp. 3–23.

Hawes, Daniel R. "The Science of Speed-Dating, Part I." *Psychology Today*, October 22, 2009. (*www.psychologytoday.com*)

Heffernan, Margaret. "Danger! Don't Hire People Just Like You." *Inc.,* January 24, 2010. (*www.inc.com*)

Hofve, Dr. Jean. "Why Cats Need Canned Food." (*www.littlebigcat.com*)

Holick, Michael F. PhD, MD, *The Vitamin D Solution*. (New York: Hudson Street Press, 2010).

Hughes, Jeff. "Study: The Truth About Online Dating Sites Selling You the Science of Love." *Digital Trends*, February 2, 2012. (*www.digitaltrends.com*)

Hughes, Susan M.; Harrison, Marissa A.; Gallup Jr., Gordon G. "Sex Differences in Romantic Kissing Among College Students: An Evolutionary Perspective." *Evolutionary Psychology*, Vol. 5, No. 3, 2007. pp. 612631. (*www.epjournal.net*)

Hurst, David. "How Watching 3D Films Can Be Bad for Your Brain." *The Daily Mail*, May 5, 2010. (*www.dailymail.co.uk*)

Jacks, G. Robert. *Getting the Word Across: Speech Communication for Pastors and Lay Leaders*. (Grand Rapids, MI: Wm. B. Eerdmans Publishing Co., 1995).

Jaffe, Chuck. "Seven Big Mistakes People Make When Hiring Advisers." *The Wall Street Journal* "Market Watch", May 20, 2010. (*http://articles.marketwatch.com*)

Jaffe, Eric. "Interview: Daniel Gilbert." *Smithsonian*, May 2007. (*www.smithsonianmag.com*)

Jervis, Lisa. *Cook Food: A Manualfesto for Easy, Healthy, Local Eating*. (Oakland, CA: PM Press, 2009).

Johnson, Rich. "Stoke Your Inner Fire: Stay Warm by Eating and Drinking the Right Stuff." *Outdoor Life*, 2010. (*www.outdoorlife.com*)

Jonath, Leslie; Slatkin, Eric; Smith, Blake. "How to Roast Vegetables with Lisa Jervis." *Chow*, February 17, 2010. (*www.chow.com*)

Kantra, Dr. David S. "A Perfect Night's Sleep." *PsychDigest*, March, 2010. (*http://psychdigest.com*)

Kaplan, Stephen. "Meditation, Restoration, and the Management of Mental Fatigue." *Environment and Behavior*, Vol. 33, No. 4, 2001, pp. 480–506.

Kappes, Heather Barry; Oettingen, Gabriele. "Positive Fantasies about Idealized Futures Sap Energy." *Journal of Experimental Social Psychology*, Vol. 47, 2011, pp. 719–729.

Katz, Mandy. "I Put in 5 Miles at the Office." *The New York Times*, September 16, 2008. (*www.nytimes.com*)

Kaufman, Scott Barry, PhD. "Speed Dating: Is It Worth Your Time?" *Psychology Today*, December 22, 2010. (*www.psychologytoday.com*)

Kelley, Charles Lee. "Coren's Turnaround: How the Pack Leader Model of Dog Training Is Flawed." *Psychology Today*, July 22, 2010. (*www.psychologytoday.com*)

Kelley, Trista. "Deaths of Headphone-Wearing Pedestrians Increase, Study Finds." *Bloomberg Businessweek*, January 20, 2012. (*www.businessweek.com*)

Kemple, Brian. "How to Dress Business Casual in the Summer." *Made Manual*, August 6, 2010. (*www.mademan.com*)

Kim, Jen. "Why Getting Revenge Isn't Worth It." *Psychology Today*, November 8, 2009. (*www.psychologytoday.com*)

Kirshenbaum, Sheril. *The Science of Kissing: What Our Lips Are Telling Us*. (New York: Grand Central Publishing, 2011).

Krasny, Jill. "Actually, Paying Off Your Smallest Debt First Is a Bad Idea." *Business Insider*, November 29, 2011. (*http://articles.businessinsider.com*)

LaBier, Douglas, PhD. "Does Imaging a Goal Make You Less Likely to Achieve It?" *Psychology Today*, July 26, 2011. (*www.psychologytoday.com*)

Lametti, Daniel. "Don't Just Sit There!" *Slate*, August 26, 2010. (*www.slate.com*)

Larkin, Marilynn. "The Power of Everyday Activity." *The New York Times*, January 8, 2008. (*www.nytimes.com*)

Larsen, Linda. "How to Measure Flour." *About.Com Busy Cooks*, (*http://busycooks.about.com*).

Laurance, Jeremy. "Scientists Debunk Decades-Old Theories on Losing Weight." *The Independent*, August 26, 2011. (*www.independent.co.uk*)

Leahy, Robert L., PhD. "Jealousy Is a Killer: How to Break Free from Your Jealous Feelings." *Psychology Today*, May 19, 2008. (*www.psychologytoday.com*)

Lee, Katie. "Calorie Restriction May Lengthen Life, but Opens Doors to Infection." *Cosmos*, July 21, 2009. (*www.cosmosmagazine.com*)

Lichenstein, Richard; Smith, Daniel Clarence; Ambrose, Jordan Lynne; Moody, Laurel Anne. "Headphone Use and Pedestrian Injury and Death in the United States: 2004–2011." *Injury Prevention*, January 16, 2012. (*http://injuryprevention.bmj.com*)

Lipman, Dr. Frank. "Make Sun Exposure Work for You." *The Huffingon Post*, July 20, 2011. (*www.huffingtonpost.com*)

Lipman, Dr. Frank. *Revive: Stop Feeling Spent and Start Living Again*. (New York: Fireside, 2009).

Liu, Alec. "5 Ways to Stay Safe on Facebook." *Fox News*, October 24, 2010. (*www.foxnews.com*)

Lohr, David. "Facebook Status Update: NH Burglary Suspects Arrested." *Aol News*, September 13, 2010. (*www.aolnews.com*)

Luccioni, LisaMarie. "How to Receive a Compliment." *Psychology Today*, March 22, 2011. (*www.psychologytoday.com*)

Lynn, Michael; Jabbour, Patrick; Kim, WooGon. "Who Uses Tips as a Reward for Service and When? An Examination of Potential Moderators of the Service-Tipping Relationship." *Journal of Economic Psychology*, Vol. 33, Issue 1, February 2012, pp. 90–103.

Lynn, Michael; McCall, Michael. "Techniques for Increasing Servers' Tips: How Generalizable Are They?" *Cornell Hospitality Quarterly*, Vol. 50, No. 2, May 2009, pp. 198–208.

Maaravi, Yossi; Ganzach, Yoav; Pazy, Asya. "Negotiation as a Form of Persuasion: Arguments in First Offers." *Journal of Personality and Social Psychology*, Vol. 101, No. 2, August 2011, pp. 245–255.

MacDonald, John. Personal interview, April 2012. (*http://macdonaldforlowell.com*)

MacPherson, Lynn. "Calorie Cycling to Lose Weight." *LiveStrong.com*, August 11, 2011.

Marano, Hara Estroff. "Jealousy: Love's Destroyer." *Psychology Today*, July 1, 2009. (*www.psychologytoday.com*)

Markman, Art, PhD. "Why We Prefer Visionary Leaders." *Psychology Today*, July 28, 2011.

Malchiodi, Cathy, PhD. "Getting Whole While Getting Even." *Psychology Today*, December 4, 2011. (*www.psychologytoday.com*)

Marangos, Paul J.; Boulenger, Jean-Philippe; Patel, Jitendra. "Effects of Chronic Caffeine on Brain Adenosine Receptors: Regional and Ontogenetic Studies." *Life Sciences*, Vol. 34, Issue 9, February 27, 1984, pp. 899–907. (*www.sciencedirect.com*)

Marjadi, Meghna. "A Walk in the Park: The New Ritalin for City Students." *The McGill Tribune*, February 16, 2009. (*www.mcgilltribune.com*)

Martin, Philip. Personal interview, April 2012. (*www.facebook.com/MartinPhilipsImaging*)

Mech, L. David. "Alpha Status, Dominance, and Division of Labor in Wolf Packs." *Canadian Journal of Zoology*, Vol. 77, 1999.

Mello Jr., John P. "Gang Uses Facebook to Rob Houses." *PC World*, September 10, 2010. (*www.pcworld.com*)

Mercola, Dr. Joseph. "This Food Can Slow Your Brain— and It Lowered IQ 4 Points in Recent Study." *Mercola.com*, January 7, 2012.

Meyer, Hilary. "4 Bad Cooking Habits You Should Break." *Eating Well*, April 25, 2011. (*www.eatingwell.com*)

Miller, Lee E.; Miller, Jessica. *A Woman's Guide to Successful Negotiating, Second Edition*. (New York: The McGraw-Hill Companies, 2011).

Mitchell, Robert L. "Online Dating: Analyzing the Algorithms of Attraction." *About.com Computing Center*, February 19, 2009. (*http://pcworld.about.net*)

Montaldo, Charles. "Stalking Statistics in the USA." *About.com Crime/Punishment*, January 2009. (*http://crime.about.com*)

Montemurri, Patricia. "Excessive Sitting Linked to Premature Death in Women." *Detroit Free Press*, reprinted in *USA Today*, August 16, 2011. (*www.usatoday.com*)

Mulkerrins, Jane. "Do 3D Films Make You Sick?" *The Telegraph*, January 11, 2010. (*www.telegraph.co.uk*)

Nachel, Marty. *Homebrewing for Dummies*. (New York: Hungry Minds, 1997).

Nase, Joseph. "Proper Serving Temperatures Are Key to Wine Enjoyment." *New York Magazine*, (*http://nymag.com*)

National Sleep Foundation, "Sleep and Lifestyle— Managing Priorities and Sleep." June 14, 2010. (*www.sleepfoundation.org*)

Neal, Rome. "Using Caffeine the Wrong Way?" *CBS News*, December 5, 2007. (*www.cbsnews.com*)

Neff, Dr. Kristin. (*www.self-compassion.org*)

Neff, Kristin. "The Chemicals of Care: How Self-Compassion Manifests in Our Bodies." *The Huffington Post*, June 27, 2011. (*www.huffingtonpost.com*)

Neff, Kristin. "Why We Should Stop Chasing Self-Esteem and Start Developing Self-Compassion." *The Huffington Post*, April 6, 2011. (*www.huffingtonpost.com*)

Nelson, Audrey, PhD. "Play Fighting: The Male Banter Game." *Psychology Today*, November 29, 2011. (*www.psychologytoday.com*)

Netterville, J.T. Personal interview, April 2012. (*Movefitness.us*)

New, Catherine. "Credit Unions Boom as Big Banks Grasp at New Fees." *The Huffington Post*, March 2, 2012. (*www.huffingtonpost.com*)

Nixon, Robin. "Brain Food: How to Eat Smart." *Live Science*, January 7, 2009. (*www.livescience.com*)

Nosowitz, Dan. "You're Doing It Wrong: How to Properly Buy, Maintain and Use a Knife." *Gizmodo*, August 31, 2009. (*http://gizmodo.com*)

Nguyen, Jenny. "Sushi Eating Tips I Learned from Mr. Yasuda." *Melting Butter*, November 15, 2010. (*http://meltingbutter.com*)

O'Connor, Anahad. "How Tanning Changes the Brain." *The New York Times*, August 12, 2011. (*http://well.blogs.nytimes.com*)

Oldham-Cooper, R.E.; Hardman, C.A.; Nicoll, C.E.; Rogers, P.J.; Brunstrom, J.M. "Playing a Computer Game During Lunch Affects Fullness, Memory for Lunch, and Later Snack Intake." *The American Journal of Clinical Nutrition*, Vol. 93, No. 2, February, 2011, pp. 308–313.

Pachter, Barbara. "Top Ten Business Clothing Mistakes." *Pachter's Pointers*, October 27, 2010. (*www.barbarapachtersblog.com*)

Pelaccio, Zakary. *Eat with Your Hands*. (New York: Ecco Publishing, 2012).

Petrecca, Laura. "Hiring Family or Friends to Work for You Can Be Boon or Bust." *USA Today*, October 15, 2010. (*www.usatoday.com*)

Pines, A. M.; Bowes, C. F. "Romantic Jealousy." *Psychology Today*, March 1, 1992. (*www.psychologytoday.com*)

Poon Tip, Bruce. Personal interview, April 2012. (*www.gadventures.com*)

Post, Emily. "General Tipping Guidelines". *Emily Post*, (*www.emilypost.com*)

Pugh, Clifford. "Fitness Enthusiasts Get a Workout Over the Web." *The Houston Chronicle*, December 13, 2000. (*www.chron.com*)

Purdy, Kevin. "What Caffeine Actually Does to Your Brain." *Lifehacker*, July 13, 2010. (*http://lifehacker.com*)

Rad, Saeed, MD. "Impact on Ethnic Habits in Defecographic Measurements." *Archives of Iranian Medicine*, Vol. 5, No. 2, April 2002. (*www.ams.ac.ir*)

Raines, Maribeth. "Methods of Sanitation and Sterilization." *Brewing Techniques*, July/August, 1993. (*http://brewingtechniques.com*)

Ray, Linda. "Nutritional Value of Roasted Vegetables." *Livestrong.com*, December 22, 2010. (*www.livestrong.com*)

Rebhahn, Peter. "Mixed Signals." *Psychology Today*, July 1, 2000. (*www.psychologytoday.com*)

REI, "Maintaining Your Bike Chain." (*www.rei.com*)

Rhoades, Heather. "Signs of Plants Affected by Too Much Water." (*www.gardeningknowhow.com*)

Richmond, Leigh A. Personal interview, April 2012. (*twitter.com/FitFunFab*)

Robinson, Sara. "Why We Have to Go Back to a 40-Hour Work Week to Keep Our Sanity." *AlterNet*, March 13, 2012. (*www.alternet.org*)

Rosen, Christine. "The Myth of Multitasking." *The New Atlantis: A Journal of Technology & Society*, Spring 2008. (*www.thenewatlantis.com*)

Rudder, Christian. "The 4 Big Myths of Profile Pictures." *Ok Cupid: Oktrends,* January 20, 2010. (*http://blog.okcupid.com*)

Ruggeri, Amanda. "15 International Food Etiquette Rules That Might Surprise You." *MSNBC News*, March 18, 2012. (*http://travelkit.msnbc.msn.com*)

Sakakibara, Ryuji; Tsunoyama, Kuniko; Hosoi, Hiroyasu; et al. "Influence of Body Position on Defecation in Humans." *Lower Urinary Tract Symptoms*, Vol. 2, Issue 1, April 2010, pp. 16–21.

Salk Institute for Biological Studies. "Key Regulator of Blood Glucose Levels Discovered." Salk News Release, September 9, 2005. (*www.salk.edu*)

Sample, Ian. "Scientists Debunk the Myth That You Lose Most Heat Through Your Head." *The Guardian*, December 17, 2008. (*www.guardian.co.uk*)

Sanchez, Don. "Are 3D Movies, TV Bad for Your Eyes?" *ABC News*, February 24, 2010. (*www.abclocal.go.com*)

Sanders, Stephanie A.; Yarber, William L.; Kaufman, Erin L.; Crosby, Richard A.; Graham, Cynthia A.; Milhausen, Robin R. "Condom Use Errors and Problems: A Global View." *Sexual Health*, Vol. 9, Issue 1, March 2, 2012, pp. 81–89.

Sbarra, David A.; Smith, Hillary L.; Mehl, Matthias R. "When Leaving Your Ex, Love Yourself: Observational Ratings of Self-Compassion Predict the Course of Emotional Recovery Following Marital Separation." *Psychological Science*, Volume 23, Issue 3, pp. 261–9. March 2012.

Searcy, Tom. "The New Rules on Dressing for Success." *CBS News*, November 8, 2011. (*www.cbsnews.com*)

Seiler, Bill. "Injuries to Headphone-Wearing Pedestrians Struck by Cars and Trains More Than Triple Since 2004." *Somnews: University of Maryland School of Medicine*, Volume 13, No. 7. January 16, 2012.

Shaw, Steven A. "Tipped Off." *The New York Times*, August 10, 2005. (*www.nytimes.com*)

Shute, Nancy. "Calories Trump Protein for Weight Loss." *National Public Radio, Shots: NPR's Health Blog*, January 4, 2012. (*www.npr.org*)

Shute, Nancy. "Working Long Hours Can Be Depressing, Truly." *National Public Radio, Shots: NPR's Health Blog*, January 26, 2012. (*www.npr.org*)

Sikirov, Dov, MD. "Comparison of Straining During Defection in Three Positions: Results and Implications for Human Health." *Digestive Diseases and Sciences,* Vol. 48, No. 7, July 2003, pp. 1201–1205.

Sisson, Mark. "Eat With Your Hands." *Mark's Daily Apple,* December 11, 2008. (*www.marksdailyapple.com*)

Sivers, Derek. "Shut Up! Announcing Your Plans Makes You Less Motivated to Accomplish Them." June 16, 2009. (*http://sivers.org*)

Slane, J.; Timmerman, M.; Ploeg, H. L.; Thelen, D. G. "The Influence of Glove and Hand Position over the Ulnar Nerve During Cycling." *Clinical Biomechanics* (Bristol, Avon), July 26, 2011, pp. 642–648.

Sleepytime Bedtime Calculator. (*http://sleepyti.me*)

Smith, Curt. "The Benefits of Speed Dating." (*www.askmen.com*)

St. James, Bethany. "Sexuality vs. Sensuality: The Steady Decline of Affection in America." *The Huffington Post,* January 10, 2012. (*www.huffingtonpost.com*)

Steenhuysen, Julie. "For Some, 3D Movies a Pain in the Head." *Reuters,* January 9, 2010. (*www.reuters.com*)

Stilwell, Victoria. *It's Me or the Dog: How to Have the Perfect Pet.* (New York: Hyperion, 2007).

Sushi Yasuda. (*www.sushiyasuda.com*)

Talley, Charlie. "Sanitation, Part Two." Basic Brewing Radio, podcast. March 29, 2007.

Tapp, Teresa. (*http://T-tapp.com*)

Toy, Vivian S. "The E-mail Handshake." *The New York Times.* April 24, 2009. (*www.nytimes.com*)

Trapani, Gina. "One Year at My Standing Desk." *Smarterware,* January 23, 2012. (*http://smarterware.org*)

Vasudev, Shefalee. "Take It Like a Man!" *Men's Health,* May, 2010.

Veronese, Keith. "What's So Bad About Sugar?" *io9*, Sept 22, 2011. (*http://io9.com*)

Videojug. "How to Tap a Keg." (*www.videojug.com/film/how-to-tap-a-keg*)

Virtanen, Marianna; Ferrie, Jane E.; Singh-Manoux, Archana; et al. "Overtime Work and Incident Coronary Heart Disease: The Whitehall II Prospective Cohort Study." *European Heart Journal*, May 11, 2010. (*http://eurheartj.oxfordjournals.org*)

Virtanen, Marianna; Stansfeld, Stephen A.; Fuhrer, Rebecca; Ferrie Jane E., Kivimäki Mika. "Overtime Work as a Predictor of Major Depressive Episode: A 5-Year Follow-Up of the Whitehall II Study." *PLoS ONE* Vol. 7, No. 1, January 25, 2012.

Von Bremzen, Anya. "Counter Culture," *Travel + Leisure*, March, 2001.

WakeMate. (*www.wakemate.com*)

Watson, Ashley. "The Produce Worker's Guide to Choosing Fruits and Vegetables." *WiseBread*, July 18, 2011. (*www.wisebread.com*)

Wax, Dustin. "How to Take a Compliment." *Stepcase Lifehack*, September 24, 2011. (*www.lifehack.org*)

Weaver, Caity. "Watch Out for 'Food Swings' When Hunger, Anger Collide." *MSNBC*, October 24, 2011. (*http://bodyodd.msnbc.msn.com*)

Webber, Rebecca. "Yes, Virginia, Some Mates Really Are Wrong." *Psychology Today*, January 1, 2012. (*www.psychologytoday.com*)

Weeks, Holly. *Failure to Communicate: How Conversations Go Wrong and What You Can Do to Right Them.* (Boston: Harvard Business School Publishing, 2008).

Weiner, Adam. "50-Minute Classroom: How to Buy Knives." (*www.cafemeetingplace.com*)

Weinstein, Norman. *Mastering Knife Skills: The Essential Guide to the Most Important Tools in Your Kitchen*. (New York: Stewart, Tabori & Chang, 2008).

Wellman, Amanda. Personal interview. April 2012. (*www.oceanvalleyvet.com*)

Whittemore, Frank. "How to Find the Right Fit Bicycle." *Livestrong.com*, July 21, 2010.

Wicklund, Robert A., Gollwitzer, Peter M. "Symbolic Self-Completion, Attempted Influence, and Self-Deprecation." *Basic and Applied Social Psychology*, Vol. 2, No. 2, 89–114, 1981, pp. 89–114.

Wyatt, James K., PhD; Cajochen, Christian, PhD; Ritz-De Cecco, Angela, et al. "Low-Dose Repeated Caffeine Administration for Circadian-Phase-Dependent Performance Degradation During Extended Wakefulness." *SLEEP*, Vol. 27, No. 3, 2004, pp. 374–381. (*www.journalsleep.org*)

Wysocki, Diane Kholos; Childers, Cheryl D. "Let My Fingers Do the Talking: Sexting and Infidelity in Cyberspace." *Sexuality & Culture*, 2011.

Yin, Sophia, DVM. (*www.drsophiayin.com*)

Young, Scott H. "How to Make Deadlines Work Using Hofstadter's Law." (*www.scottyoung.com*)

Zwilling, Martin. "Startups, Avoid 10 Common Million-Dollar Mistakes." *Forbes*, August 11, 2011. (*www.forbes.com*)

# Index

**A**

Abs, flattening, 35–36
Aguilera, Adrian, 174
Amar, Moty, 143–44
*American Idol*, 69
Aniston, Jennifer, 118
*Annoying: The Science of What Bugs Us*, 85
Armstrong, Lance, 32
*The Art of Singing*, 69
*Avatar*, 62
Ayoob, Keith, 31

**B**

Baker, Fred, 141
Banks, Martin, 60
Barreca, Regina, 65
Bartlett, Griffin, 198
Bashir, Waseem Amir, 50
Baume, Matthew, 33–34
Beer, homebrewing, 98–100
Beer keg, tapping, 113–15
Berard, Guy, 27
*The Berkeley Science Review*, 38
Bettcher, Jessica, 81
*Betty's Book of Laundry Secrets*, 188
Beverage tips, 16–17, 98–100, 110–15
Bike riding, 32–34

Blumer, Bob, 122
Bonné, Jon, 111–12
*Boy's Life*, 191
Bradshaw, John, 194
Branson, Richard, 129
Breakup, handling, 164–66
Brinkley, Douglas, 132
Brockovitch, Erin, 127
Bukunt, Jeffrey, 54
Bushman, B . J., 64–65
Business casual, wearing, 125–27
Business/finance tips, 123–58
Buss, David, 168

**C**

Calories, restricting, 40–41
Cameron, James, 62
Carlsmith, Kevin, 64, 65
Carroll, Aaron E., 42
Carter, Jimmy, 44
Cat, feeding, 195–97
Cell phone etiquette, 83–85
Chanel, Coco, 20
Chansky, Tamar, 68
Chase, Raluca, 80
Chavez, Amy, 46
Choi, Roy, 120
Chow, Carson, 41

*Chromatics*, 80

*Clash of the Titans*, 62

Coakley, Jay, 68

Coffee, drinking, 16–17

Cohen, Randy, 85

Compliments, 74–76

Conversing, 57–59

*Cook Food*, 104

Cooking tips, 93–97,
    101–9, 120–22

Corson, Trevor, 107

Coryate, Thomas, 121

Cowell, Simon, 67

Coyne, Sarah, 174–75

Crane, Robert Morrison, 28

Crannell, Kenneth, 77, 78

Credit cards, paying off,
    143–45


**D**

Dating, online, 179–81

Dating, speed, 182–83

Deadlines, facing, 131–33

Debt, paying off, 143–45

Dog, training, 192–94

*Dog Sense*, 194

*Dog Whisperer with Cesar
    Millan*, 192

Dunn, Elizabeth, 149


**E**

*The Early Show*, 17

Earphones, wearing, 26–28

Eastwick, Paul, 180

Ebert, Roger, 61–62

*The Economist*, 132

Employees, hiring, 128–30

*Entrepreneur*, 130

*Evolutionary Psychology*, 162

Exercise, and sitting, 23–25

Exercise tips, 18–19, 23–25,
    32–36. *See also* Fitness tips


**F**

Facebook, updating, 53–56

*Failure to Communicate*, 58

Faust, Betty, 188

Feuerman, Simon, 75

Field, George, 80

Finance tips, 123–58

Finkel, Eli, 180

Fitness tips, 11–50

Flagg, Donna, 57

Flanagan, Sinead, 179

Flour, measuring, 93–94

Food tips, 91–97, 101–9,
    116–22

Ford, Henry, 138

*Freeing Your Child from
    Negative Thinking*, 68

Freilich, Michael, 44

Fun/social tips, 51–89


**G**

Germs, avoiding, 13–15

Gilbert, Daniel T., 64–65,
    70–71, 149

Goals, sharing, 71–73

Goldman, Leslie, 68
Gollwitzer, Peter M., 72
Gordon, Amie, 38
Grimes, William, 108

## H
Hamady, Jennifer, 69
Happiness, buying, 149–52
Headphones, wearing, 26–28
Health tips, 11–50
Heineman, Rick, 61
Herbert, George, 64
Hiring people, 128–30
Hofstadter, Douglas, 132
Hofstadter's Law, 131–32
Hofve, Jean, 197
Holick, Michael F., 21, 22
Homebrewing beer, 98–100
*Homebrewing for Dummies*, 99
Home tips, 185–200
*Huffington Post*, 141, 163, 173

## I
*It's Me or the Dog!*, 193

## J
Jacks, G. Robert, 79
James, William, 134
Jaminet, Paul, 30
*The Japan Times*, 46

Jealousy, handling, 167–69
Jervis, Lisa, 104
Johnson, Rich, 43

## K
Kantra, David S., 37
Kaplan, Stephen, 134–35
Kappes, Heather Barry, 157
Kardashian, Kim, 78
Kaufman, Scott Barry, 183
Keg, tapping, 113–15
Keller, Helen, 84
Kerouac, Jack, 133
King, Carole, 27
Kira, Alexander, 44
Kirshenbaum, Sheril, 161
Kissing tips, 161–63
Kivimäki, Mika, 138
Knives, choosing, 101–3

## L
LaBier, Douglas, 158
LaLanne, Jack, 23
Larsen, Linda, 94
Lawn, caring for, 198–200
Levine, James A., 24
Lichenstein, Richard, 26
Lichtman, Flora, 85
Lipman, Frank, 21
Lohr, David, 54
Lombardi, Vince, 68, 69
Luccioni, LisaMarie, 75–76
Lynn, Michael, 118

## M

MacDonald, John, 141
Magid, Larry, 84
Mahler, Wera, 72
Malchiodi, Cathy, 65
Marano, Hara Estroff, 168
Martin, Philip, 80
McCubbin, Boris, 54
McCubbin, Claudette, 54
McGraw, Elizabeth, 41
McMullen, Keri, 54
Mead, G. H., 72
*Men's Health*, 76
Meyer, Danny, 85
Millan, Cesar, 192
Miller, Lee E., 154
Money, saving, 140–42
Movies, watching, 60–62
Multitasking, 146–48
Murch, Walter, 61–62
Murphy's Law, 131

## N

Nachel, Marty, 99
Nase, Joseph, 110–11
Nass, Clifford, 147, 148
Neff, Kristin, 165
Negotiating, 153–55
Netterville, J. T., 18, 35
*Newsweek*, 68
*New York* magazine, 110
*New York Times*, 85, 108, 120

## O

Oettingen, Gabriele, 157
Oldham-Cooper, R. E., 148
Online dating, 179–81
Ophir, Eyal, 147
*Outdoor Life*, 43

## P

Parkinson, Cyril, 132
Parkinson's Law, 132
Partner, texting, 173–75
*PC World*, 180
Pendleton, Kurt, 54
*Peter Rabbit*, 63
Pets, feeding, 195–97
Pets, training, 192–94
Pictures, taking, 80–82
Poon Tip, Bruce, 86–88
Pooping, 44–46
Positive manifestations, 156–58
Post, Emily, 117, 119
Produce, choosing, 95–97
Productivity, increasing, 134–36
*PsychDigest*, 37
*Psychology Today*, 65, 69, 158, 168

## R

Rad, Saeed, 45
Ramsay, Gordon, 98

Real, Terrence, 172
Relationship, working on, 170–72
Relationship tips, 159–83
Repole, Mike, 130
Resources, 120
Restaurants, tipping, 116–19
Revenge, getting, 63–66
Richmond, Leigh A., 40
Rick, Scott, 143–44
Rodale, Maria, 188
Rosenberg, Michael, 61

## S

Safe sex, 176–78
Sahni, Julie, 122
Sakakibara, Ryuji, 45
Samuelsson, Marcus, 122
Saving money, 140–42
Sbarra, David, 164–65
Scantling, Sandra, 161
*Science Daily*, 174
Senay, Emily, 17
Sex tips, 159–63, 176–78
Sexton, Jonathan, 14
Sikirov, Dov, 45
Sisson, Mark, 122
Sitting, and exercise, 23–25
Sitting, posture for, 49–50
*Sleep* (journal), 17
Sleep, timing, 37–39

*Smithsonian*, 70
Social/fun tips, 51–89
Social networking, 53–56
Speaking tips, 77–79
Spears, Britney, 78
Speed dating, 182–83
Spot training, 18–19
Stains, removing, 187–89
STDs, protecting against, 176–78
Stemmer, Phil, 47
Stevens, Cat, 27
Stilwell, Victoria, 193–94
St. James, Bethany, 163
*The Story of Sushi*, 107
*Stumbling on Happiness*, 70
Sugar, cutting, 29–31
*Surviving Dreaded Conversations*, 57
Sushi, eating, 107–9

## T

Talley, Charlie, 99
Tanning, 20–22
Tapp, Teresa, 35–36
Teeth, brushing, 47–48
Texting partner, 173–75
3D movies, 60–62
Tila, Jet, 122
*Time* magazine, 44
Tipping, 116–19
*Titanic*, 62

Traveling internationally, 86–89
Trump, Donald, 130
Twain, Mark, 85
Tweeting, 53–56
Twitter, 54–55

## U

*Urban Dictionary*, 31
*USA Today*, 130
Utensils, using, 120–22

## V

Vasudev, Shefalee, 76
Vegetables, roasting, 104–6
Virtanen, Marianna, 138
Visualization, 156–58
*The Vitamin D Solution*, 21
Vreeman, Rachel C., 42

## W

WakeMate, 38
Walkstation, 24
Warm, staying, 42–43
Wax, Dustin, 76
WD-40 tips, 190–91
Weeks, Holly, 58
Weil, Andrew, 21
Weinstein, Norman, 102
Wellman, Amanda, 195
Whittemore, Frank, 33

Wicklund, Robert A., 72
Wilson, Timothy, 64, 65, 149
Wine, serving, 110–12
Winning, 67–70
Working long hours, 137–39
Working out, 18–19, 23–25, 35–36. *See also* Fitness tips
Work tips, 123–58
Wyatt, James K., 17

## Y

Yasuda, Naomichi, 108